Making
Vocational Choices

**PRENTICE-HALL SERIES IN
COUNSELING AND HUMAN DEVELOPMENT**

Norman R. Stewart, *Consulting Editor*

Making
Vocational Choices

a theory of careers

JOHN L. HOLLAND

Johns Hopkins University

Prentice-Hall, Inc., Englewood Cliffs, New Jersey

Library of Congress Cataloging in Publication Data

Holland, John L
   Making vocational choices.

   Bibliography: p.
   1. Vocational guidance. I. Title.
HF5381.H5668   331.7'02   73-4847
ISBN   0-13-547828-6
ISBN   0-13-547810-3 (pbk.)

TO ELSIE

Printed in the United States of America

20 19 18 17 16 15 14 13 12 11

Acknowledgment–Appendixes A, B, and C (pages
107-131) were reproduced by special permission
from Consulting Psychologists Press, Inc.

Prentice-Hall International, Inc., London
Prentice-Hall of Australia, Pty. Ltd., Sydney
Prentice-Hall of Canada, Ltd., Toronto
Prentice-Hall of India Private Limited, New Delhi
Prentice-Hall of Japan, Inc., Tokyo

Contents

Preface

I have written this book to present a theory of careers that I hope practitioners, researchers, and students will find useful in vocational counseling, education, and social science. And although I have written primarily for a graduate student and professional audience, I have tried to write so that an intelligent person can, without much difficulty, find the principal ideas clear and helpful.

To accomplish these goals, I have presented the theory as directly as I could and without the customary asides, doubts, and cautions. These traditional misgivings are summarized instead in Chapter 5, "Some Evidence," along with the findings on the usefulness of the theory. With the exception of this technical summary, the rest of the book is usually in plain English. By separating the statement of the theory from the evidence, all readers should find it easier to comprehend and to evaluate.

This book is my third formulation of the theory. The first was a journal article based largely upon my experience as a vocational counselor and as a reader of the vocational literature (Holland, 1959). This first a priori formulation led to some encouraging research, so that a second and more systematic formulation became possible—a brief book (Holland, 1966b). The little book was written to provide more explicit definitions of the main concepts, to provide more comprehensive formulations, and to attract the help of other researchers. Much to my surprise, other researchers appeared, and more than a hundred studies of the theory's usefulness have now been performed.

This third statement offers a theory that better complies with scientific standards of logic and evidence, and suggests some concrete applications. The theory is now more properly a theory of careers, for it deals more completely and successfully with vocational problems throughout a person's life: vocational choice, work history, job changes, occupational achievement.

Compared with the earlier statements, the present one is more comprehensive and systematic. In general, the theory has been tidied up. A few hypotheses have been deleted for lack of support; others have been deleted because they represented unnecessary burdens for any theory to bear. The outcomes or human behaviors that the theory is directed toward have been made more complete, and these outcomes are dealt with more consistently. Most important, the theory has been restructured so that it has both a clearer structure and a simpler statement. These revisions should make it easier to comprehend, to evaluate in research, and to apply to everyday problems.

The theory is in the tradition of typologies of personality, but it differs from nearly all earlier typologies in many ways: (1) The typology has been revised in response to data. (2) It is a typology of persons *and* environments. (3) Degrees and patterns of resemblance to models have been substituted for all-or-none distinctions among types so that the theory can cope more successfully with the complexity of human behavior. (4) An attempt has been made to cope with the processes of development, stability, and change in accordance with the simpler concepts of learning theory. (5) All major concepts have been given empirical definition. And (6) a single spatial model (a hexagon) has been used to coordinate all the concepts in the theory. In short, we may be wrong, but we are clear!

I am indebted to many friends and colleagues who have provided me with valuable counsel and criticism in writing this book. They include Charles F. Elton, Thomas T. Frantz, Beulah M. Hedahl, James M. Richards, Jr., Keith F. Taylor, W. Bruce Walsh, Douglas R. Whitney, Samuel T. Helms, Dean H. Nafziger, and Michael S. Swafford.

I am also indebted to John H. Hollifield for his ability to recast my writing into plain English. I am especially grateful to William A. Alston, whose skillful tutoring about philosophical matters has been instrumental in reshaping the theory so that it has a more felicitous form. It was under his guidance that I simplified and restructured the theory so that it would conform more to scientific standards.

I remain obligated to many other colleagues who helped me at earlier stages of this venture. They include Alexander W. Astin, Leonard L. Baird, John D. Black, Thomas M. Magoon, Samuel H. Osipow, Donald P. Hoyt, Robert C. Nichols, John M. Stalnaker, Donald L. Thistlethwaite, Nancy S. Cole, Mary Cowan Viernstein, Harold F. Giedt, William G. Fairweather, and Thelma Baldwin Zener.

These and other colleagues have provided so much help for such a long time that I can no longer discriminate their ideas from my own or always remember their special contribution. I am in their debt for much of what is useful in this book.

Like alcoholics or artists, researchers need sponsors. I have been fortunate to have had sponsors who have at least tolerated my hobby and delusional system from 1953 to 1972. They have included Case-Western Reserve University, Consulting Psychologists Press, the Veterans Administration, the National Merit Scholarship Corporation, the National Science Foundation, the Carnegie Corporation of New York, the American College Testing Program, the Federal Office of Education, and Johns Hopkins University. Needless to say, neither my past nor present employers endorse the ideas presented here.

Towson, Maryland   JOHN L. HOLLAND

Introduction to the Theory

chapter 1

Everyone has vocational decisions to make and vocational problems to resolve. At various stages of life we must deal with vocational decisions, problems, or stresses: What do I want to be when I grow up? Should I become an electrician or a teacher? Should I become a secretary or an accountant? I am a good research engineer, but should I accept a supervisory job? I dislike my job, but why? I am 45 and dissatisfied—what would be a satisfying second career? I have never been a good salesman; have I missed the boat somewhere? I got fired—why? How can I make my retirement more fulfilling?

Everyone must also serve as a vocational coach. With or without appropriate training, parents, teachers, employers, counselors, friends, and others are confronted with numerous coaching problems. What are the best ways to help people make satisfying vocational decisions? What educational programs are needed? What special programs are needed for poor people? What can be done to help women resolve their vocational difficulties? How can jobs be made more satisfying or fulfilling?

The questions raised by players and coaches are what this book is about. It summarizes much of what we know about careers and presents a special way of organizing and interpreting this knowledge for easier comprehension and practical application—in short, a theory. Specifically, this theory consists of a set of rules and definitions that can be used to understand persons and environments, especially people in different occupations and their occupational environments. Like in a game, the reader has to learn the rules before he can use the theory.

The primary concern of the theory is to explain vocational behavior and suggest some practical ideas to help young, middle-aged, and older people select jobs, change jobs, and attain vocational satisfaction. To a lesser degree, the theory also concerns personal competence, educational behavior, and social behavior. The inclusion of these areas is the natural outcome of the development of the theory as it has acquired greater clarity of statement and more evidence for a wider range of usefulness. The following section summarizes the main ideas. The remainder of the book elaborates these ideas, summarizes the scientific evidence for their validity, and shows how to apply them to selected vocational, personnel, and educational problems.

A SUMMARY OF THE THEORY

The theory consists of several simple ideas and their more complex elaborations. First, we can characterize people by their resemblance to each of six personality types: realistic, investigative, artistic, social, enterprising, and conventional. The more closely a person resembles a particular type, the more likely he is to exhibit the personal traits and behaviors associated with that type. Second, the environments in which people live can be characterized by their resemblance to six model environments: realistic, investigative, artistic, social, enterprising, and conventional. Finally, the pairing of persons and environments leads to outcomes that we can predict and understand from our knowledge of the personality types and the environmental models. These outcomes include vocational choice, vocational stability and achievement, educational choice and achievement, personal competence, social behavior, and susceptibility to influence.

Four working assumptions constitute the heart of the theory. They indicate the nature of the personality types and environmental models, how the types and models are determined, and how they interact to create the phenomena—vocational, educational, and social—that the theory is meant to explain.

1. In our culture, most persons can be categorized as one of six types: realistic, investigative, artistic, social, enterprising, or conventional. The description of each type (see Chapter 2) is both a summary of what we know about people in a given occupational group and a special way of comprehending this information: It is a theoretical or ideal type. A *type* is a model against which we can measure the real person.

Each type is the product of a characteristic interaction between a variety of cultural and personal forces, including peers, parents, social class, culture, and the physical environment. Out of this experience, a person learns first to prefer some activities as opposed to others. Later, these activities become strong interests. Such interests lead to a special group of competencies. Finally, a person's interests and competencies create a particular personal disposition that leads him to think, perceive, and act in special ways. For example, if a person resembles the social type, he is more likely to seek out social occupations such as teaching, social work, or the ministry. He would be expected to see himself as social and friendly. He would be expected to have more social competencies (such as helping others with personal problems) than realistic competencies (such as using tools or understanding machines). He would value socially oriented problems or tasks: helping others, serving his community, upholding religion.

By comparing a person's attributes with those of each model type, we can determine which type he resembles most. That model becomes his *personality type*. Then we can also determine what other types he resembles. For example, a person might resemble a social type most, then an enterprising type, then the other types in descending order. His total resemblance to each of the six types forms a pattern of similarity and dissimilarity—the person's *personality pattern*. Thus we obtain a profile of resemblances that allows for the complexity of personality and avoids some of the problems inherent in categorizing a person as a single type. A six-category scheme built on the assumption that there are only six kinds of people in the world is unacceptable on the strength of common sense alone. But a six-category scheme that allows a simple ordering of a person's resemblance to each of the six models provides the possibility of 720 different personality patterns.

To estimate a person's profile or personality pattern, we can use one of several methods: a person's scores on selected scales from interest and personality inventories, his choice of vocation or field of training, his work history or his history of preemployment aspirations, or combinations of these data. For example, certain scales of the Vocational Preference Inventory, the Strong Vocational Interest Blank, and the Self-directed Search have been designated as estimates of the types. The procedure is to have a person take an inventory, score it, and profile the appropriate scales. The profiles can then be interpreted by applying the descriptions of the types.

2. There are six kinds of environments: realistic, investigative, artistic, social, enterprising, and conventional. Each environment is dominated by a given type of personality, and each environment is typified by physical settings posing special problems and stresses. For example, realistic environments are "dominated" by realistic types of people—that is, the largest percentage of the population in the realistic environment resembles the realistic type. A conventional environment is dominated by conventional types.

Because different types have different interests, competencies, and dispositions, they tend to surround themselves with special people and materials and to seek out problems that are congruent with their interests, competencies, and outlook on the world. Thus, where people congregate, they create an environment that reflects the types they are, and it becomes possible to assess the environment in the same terms as we assess people individually. One method of accomplishing this task is to count the number of different types in an environment. The distribution of types is then converted to percentages of the total number of people in the environment. The environment is represented by six percentages and is interpreted by the environmental formulations given in Chapter 3.

3. People search for environments that will let them exercise their skills and abilities, express their attitudes and values, and take on agreeable problems and roles. Realistic types seek realistic environments, social types seek social environments, and so forth. To a lesser extent, environments also search for people through friendships and recruiting practices. The person's search for environments is carried on in many ways, at different levels of consciousness, and over a long period of time. The personality types epitomize some common ways in which people develop in our culture. They also illustrate how personal development channels goals, vocational choices, and mobility.

4. A person's behavior is determined by an interaction between his personality and the characteristics of his environment. If we know a person's personality pattern and the pattern of his environment, we can, in principle, use our knowledge of personality types and environmental models to forecast some of the outcomes of such a pairing. Such outcomes include choice of vocation, job changes, vocational achievement, personal competence, and educational and social behavior.

These four key assumptions are supplemented by several secondary assumptions that can be applied to both a person and his environment. These include the following:

Consistency. Within a person or an environment, some pairs of types are more closely related than others. For example, realistic-investigative have more in common than conventional-artistic. And degrees of consistency or relatedness are assumed to affect vocational preference—realistic-investigative should be more predictable than realistic-social.

Differentiation. Some persons or environments are more clearly defined than others. For instance, a person may closely resemble a single type and show little resemblance to other types, or an environment may be dominated largely by a single type. In contrast, a person who resembles many types or an environment that is characterized by about equal numbers of the six types would be labeled undifferentiated or poorly defined.

Congruence. Different types require different environments. For instance, realistic types flourish in realistic environments because such an environment provides the opportunities and rewards a realistic type needs. Incongruence occurs when a type lives in an environment that provides opportunities and rewards foreign to the person's preferences and abilities—for instance, a realistic type in a social environment.

Calculus. The relationships within and between types or environments can be ordered according to a hexagonal model in which the distances between the types or environments are inversely proportional to the theoretical relationships between them. This spatial arrangement provides explicit definitions of both consistency (three levels) and congruence of person and environment (three or more). In this way, the internal relationships of the theory are defined and organized by a single geometrical model (see Figure 3, page 23).

The secondary concepts have two purposes: to improve the predictions obtained by the main concepts and to substitute degrees of consistency, differentiation, and congruence for the all-or-none definitions of the same concepts provided earlier (Holland, 1966b).

BACKGROUND CONCEPTS AND ORIGINS

The present theory comes from and rests upon the work of many others. This section provides a brief account of the main origins of the theory and some additional background principles that I have proposed or borrowed from others. These ideas are important to the theory, but usually less so than the main ideas summarized earlier.

Origins

The formulations for the types grew out of my experience as a vocational counselor in educational, military, and psychiatric settings. That experience, the vocational literature, and the construction of the Vocational Preference Inventory (Holland, 1958) gradually led me to the notion that it might be helpful to categorize people in terms of interest or personality types. (The VPI is shown in Appendix A.)

The idea for a typology resulted from my frequently observing—and the observations of others as well—that several broad classes account for most human interests, traits, and behaviors. In a now obscure article, Darley (1938) had suggested the potential value of organizing our knowledge according to occupational stereotypes. As a beginning, I used six scales of the Vocational Preference Inventory that correspond to the present personality types: realistic, investigative, artistic, social, enterprising, and conventional. Somewhat later, I was impressed and reassured by Guilford's (1954) comprehensive factor analysis of human interest in which he obtained six major factors to account for the diversity of interests and personality traits: mechanical, scientific, social welfare, clerical, business, and esthetic. To the best of my knowledge, Guilford's factor analysis is the most explicit forerunner of the present typology.

The present types are analogous in some ways to the types proposed earlier by Adler (1939), Fromm (1947), Jung (1933), Sheldon (1954), Spranger (1928), and others. They differ from these earlier typologies in their origin (which is largely the vocational literature) and in their empirical definitions (see Chapter 2). In addition, I have tried to formulate a clear testable structure for each type and to conform with as many scientific principles of logic and evidence as possible.

The notion of assessing environments by characterizing the people in a particular environment came from Linton (1945), who suggested that a major portion of the force of the environment is transmitted through other people. The typology thus became a method for engineering Linton's idea—that is, by calculating the distribution of types in an environment, you will know the environment. This hypothesis led to the development of the Environmental Assessment Technique (Astin and Holland, 1961), which has been used to describe college environments.

The assumption that human behavior depends upon *both* personality and the specific environment in which a person lives has a long history. However, Murray's formulations (1938) of personal "needs" and environmental "pressures" were the immediate stimulus for the use of personality types and environmental models here.

Throughout the development and study of the theory, I have been impressed with the need for pragmatism. Any research study requires much time and resources, so I have tried to limit the use of the theory to simple, inexpensive, practical definitions and measures. Further, I have hoped that the elaboration of these simple approaches would be sufficient to cope with much of the complexity of human behavior and human environments.

Background Principles

In developing the typology and the environmental models, a number of principles seemed plausible, or at least hard to imagine as false. These are enumerated below, along with some arguments for their acceptance.

The choice of a vocation is an expression of personality. For many years it was popular to interpret a person's scores on vocational interest inventories and his choice of vocation as a function of his "vocational interests," as if these interests were different from or independent of personality. A long history of adherence to this concept produced an independent literature known as "interest measurement." Some of the work of Strong (1943), Super and Crites (1962), and Campbell (1971) epitomizes the view that vocational interests measure only interests, vocational choices, and vocational preferences.

Recent knowledge about the personal and environmental factors associated with vocational choice, job changes, and vocational achievement has revealed the need for a broader conception. We have learned that vocational preferences are sometimes moderately correlated with personality and originality scales (Holland, 1963), self-ratings of ability and personality traits and life goals (Baird, 1970), parental attitudes (Medvene, 1969), objective perceptual tests (Crutchfield, Woodworth and Albrecht, 1958), and many other psychological and sociological variables. For many years, writers have suggested the need for a more comprehensive view of vocational preferences and interests: "Interest inventory scores are measures of self-concept" (Bordin, 1943); "vocational interest measurement is a special case in personality theory" (Darley and Hagenah, 1955); "vocational choice is a developmental process" and is, in large part, "the implementation of a person's self-concept" (Super, 1972). These orientations consistently imply that a person's vocational interests flow from his life history and his personality.

If vocational interests are construed as an expression of personality, then they represent the expression of personality in work, school subjects, hobbies, recreational activities, and preferences. In short, what we have called "vocational interests" are simply another aspect of personality. Just as we have developed theories of personality from our knowledge of sex and parental relationships, so we can construct theories of personality from our knowledge of vocational life. We can then reinterpret vocational interests as an expression of personality. The theory is mainly an elaborate engineering of this key idea.

Interest inventories are personality inventories. If vocational interests are an expression of personality, then it follows that interest inventories are personality inventories. Forer (1948) was probably the first to develop an inventory to assess personality from interests and activities, and to illustrate how a subject's responses to apparently neutral content (vocational interests and activities) could be interpreted as expressions of various dimensions of personality. Although Forer did not put his ideas to a direct scientific test, he did show that we can distinguish a great variety of medical and psychiatric groups (asthmatics to schizophrenics) by their scores on various scales of one interest inventory, the Kuder Preference Record (Forer, 1951). Forer's theorizing led to the construction of Holland's Vocational Preference Inventory (1958, 1965), a personality inventory composed entirely of occupational titles. In general, the scales were developed by hypothesizing that preferences for occupations are expressions of personality. The rationale for the development of the inventory contains a more complete statement of this hypothesis:

> The choice of an occupation is an expressive act which reflects the
> person's motivation, knowledge, personality, and ability.
> Occupations represent a way of life, an environment rather than a
> set of isolated work functions or skills. To work as a carpenter
> means not only to use tools but also to have a certain status,
> community role, and a special pattern of living. In this sense, the
> choice of an occupational title represents several kinds of
> information: the S's motivation, his knowledge of the occupation in

question, his insight and understanding of himself, and his abilities. In short, item responses may be thought of as limited but useful expressive or projective protocols (Holland, 1965, p. 2).

The development and validation of the Vocational Preference Inventory make it clear that vocational preferences are indeed signs of personality traits. Recent work by Baird (1970), Campbell (1971), and others also shows that interest scales are positively related to a person's values, academic achievement, liberalism, adventurousness, and other personal characteristics.

To summarize, it seems useful to interpret vocational interest inventories as personality inventories. Moreover, the content of vocational interest inventories provides scales whose reliabilities and validities approximate those obtained for other methods for assessing personality.

Vocational stereotypes have reliable and important psychological and socio-logical meanings. Just as we judge people by their friends, dress, and actions, so we judge them by their vocations. Our everyday experience has generated a sometimes inaccurate but apparently useful knowledge of what people in various occupations are like. Thus we believe that plumbers are handy, lawyers aggressive, actors self-centered, salesmen persuasive, accountants precise, scientists unsociable, and the like. In earlier years, social scientists were skeptical of the accuracy of this amorphous folklore of vocational stereotypes (some still are), but recent work makes it clear that many have some validity.

O'Dowd and Beardslee (1960, 1967) have demonstrated that occupations are perceived in much the same way by high school students, college students, college faculty, and men versus women. They also found that demographic differences (that is, a person's social status) make only small differences in the perception of occupations and that occupational stereotypes change only slightly during four years of college. Most recently, Marks and Webb (1969) demonstrated that students entering the fields of industrial management or electrical engineering possess "a fairly accurate image—assuming the pro-fessionals know what they are talking about—of the typical incumbent of the intended occupation." Their elaborate study of two occupational titles by three levels of experience—freshmen, seniors, and professionals before, during, and after training—practically closes the door on the argument that inexperienced and experienced people do not see an occupation in the same way.

This finding has considerable and pervasive importance for vocational behavior. Most interest inventories rest heavily on the assumptions that people perceive occupations and their associated activities accurately and that these perceptions remain the same over long periods of time. In the same way, a person's vocational preferences and choices rest on the same assumptions. If perceptions of occupations had no validity, interest inventories would have little or no validity.

The members of a vocation have similar personalities and similar histories of personal development. If a person enters a given vocation because of his particular personality and history, it follows that each vocation attracts and retains people with similar personalities. Laurent's study of engineers, physicians, and lawyers (1951) documents the similarities in life histories for the members of a vocation. Other studies—for example, Roe (1956), Kulberg and Owens (1960), Chaney and Owens (1964), and Nachmann (1960)—lend support to this assumption. And, if we should form classes made up of vocations demanding similar personalities, we would get groups of people who are alike. For example, groups of scientists such as physicists, chemists, and mathematicians should be grossly similar, because the evidence indicates that physical scientists have something in common.

Because people in a vocational group have similar personalities, they will respond to many situations and problems in similar ways, and they will create characteristic interpersonal environments. Although we cannot test this assumption directly, we do have some indirect evidence. For example, Astin and Holland (1961) were able to predict what college students would say about their college and about fellow students. The method entails a simple census of the number of students in each of six curricular groups: realistic, investigative, social, conventional, enterprising, and artistic. The percentage of students in each curricular group at a given college becomes the profile of that college. In that first study, Astin and Holland found, for example, that the percentage of students in the realistic group was correlated with a student's description of the college and its students as pragmatic rather than humanistic. It is possible then to describe a college by a simple census of its members if one has a way to interpret the meaning of membership in various curriculums. More recent studies (Astin, 1968; Richards, Seligman, and Jones, 1970) have validated these ideas in large-scale analyses of educational environments.

Vocational satisfaction, stability, and achievement depend on the congruence between one's personality and the environment (composed largely of other people) in which one works. Just as we are more comfortable among friends whose tastes, talents, and values are similar to our own, so we are more likely to perform well at a vocation in which we "fit" psychologically. The Strong and other generally accepted vocational inventories are based in part on this assumption. Moreover, the vocational literature is filled with evidence that supports the assumption, although that evidence is not usually interpreted as relating to the interaction between a particular personality and a particular environment. In the present theory, the congruence of a person and his environment is defined in terms of the *structure* of personality types and environmental models. For example, a person is in a congruent or fitting environment when the environment calls for the activities he prefers, demands his special competencies, and reinforces his personal disposition and its associated characteristics—a special outlook on the world, role preferences, values, and personal traits.

SUMMARY

The present chapter outlines a theory of careers and some of its origins and key assumptions. The following chapters offer a more complete exposition. Chapter 2, "The Personality Types," provides detailed descriptions of the theoretical types and their expected performance. Chapter 3 specifies The Environmental Models. Chapter 4, "People in Environments," shows what happens when different personalities live in different environments, and Chapter 5 summarizes the evidence for the usefulness of the theory. Finally, Chapter 6 outlines the practical applications of the theory to personal, educational, and industrial problems.

The Personality Types

chapter 2

This chapter provides the theoretical formulations for each of the six personality types. Separate sections summarize how types develop, what each type is like, how types are assessed, how types resemble one another, and how types behave.

DEVELOPMENT OF TYPES

The purpose of this section is to outline how personality types develop and to do so in the context of the formulations for the types. These speculative statements are intended to make the theory more complete and to facilitate its study and application. Each type is assumed to develop according to the following formula: To some degree, types produce types. Although parental attitudes play a minor and complex role in the development of a child's interests (Roe, 1956; Roe and Siegelman, 1964; Medvene, 1969), the assumption here is that each parental type provides a large cluster of environmental opportunities, as well as some deficits which extend well beyond parental attitudes. For example, realistic parents (their child-rearing attitudes aside) engage in characteristic realistic activities in and out of the home; surround themselves with particular equipment, possessions, materials, and tools; and select realistic friends and neighborhoods. At the same time, realistic parents tend to ignore, avoid, or reject some activities and types more than others. For instance, realistic parents will be expected to reject social activities, people, and situations. In short, parents create characteristic environments that include attitudes as well as a great range of obvious environmental experiences.

Further, children create their own environment to a limited degree by their demands upon parents and by the manner in which parents react to and are influenced by children (Bell, 1968). Presumably, the more a child resembles a particular parent, the more reward he will receive—so parent-child relationships, like other personal relationships, may demonstrate that types are attracted to types. When parental and child data are organized in the typology, positive associations among types should occur because large clusters of characteristic activities, competencies, vocational preferences, and so on are being assessed, not just subtle attitudes that can be easily distorted by the assessment process and that constitute only a small portion of the multiple and varied influences parents exert.

By using parental personality patterns and the secondary concepts of consistency and differentiation, the clarity and intensity of parental influence can be estimated. In addition, the combined effect of both parents can be estimated by ascertaining the congruity between parental personality patterns using Cole's planar method (Cole and Cole, 1970) or the hexagonal model. See Figure 3, page 23.

A child's special heredity and experience first lead to preferences for some kinds of activities and aversions to others. Later, these preferences become well-defined interests from which the person gains self-satisfaction as well as reward from others. Still later, the pursuit of these interests leads to the development of more specialized competencies as well as to the neglect of other potential competencies. At the same time, a person's differentiation of interests with age is accompanied by a crystallization of correlated values. These events—an increasing differentiation of preferred activities, interests, competencies, and values—create a characteristic disposition or personality type that is predisposed to exhibit characteristic behavior and to develop characteristic personality traits. These include:

1. Self-concepts
2. Perception of the environment
3. Values
4. Achievement and performance
5. Differential reaction to environmental rewards, stress, and so on
6. Preference for occupation and occupational role
7. Coping style
8. Personal traits

This simplified account of personality development avoids any consideration of the complex and involuted ways in which personality is usually assumed to develop. The simplification is achieved by limiting the account to a general discussion of easily observed developments. These events *do* happen and, for the purposes of this theory, that is sufficient. Thus we can substitute a straightforward account of activities, competencies, values, and interests for a more complex model of sex, siblings, and parental relationships. The simple model will, we hope, provide a useful form for explaining some human behavior without the usual complexities.

Figure 1 illustrates how types may develop. To summarize, some of a child's initial activities lead to long-term interests and competencies. That experience creates a person who is predisposed to exhibit a characteristic self-concept and outlook and to acquire a characteristic group of traits. This general formula is used to structure the formulations in the next section.

FORMULATIONS OF THE TYPES

The types are assumed to represent common outcomes of growing up in our culture. Each type is described in terms of a theoretical model created with several goals in mind: (1) To outline only the bare bones of the experiences that lead to a particular kind of person; (2) to show how a person's experience leads

FIGURE 1
How Types May Develop

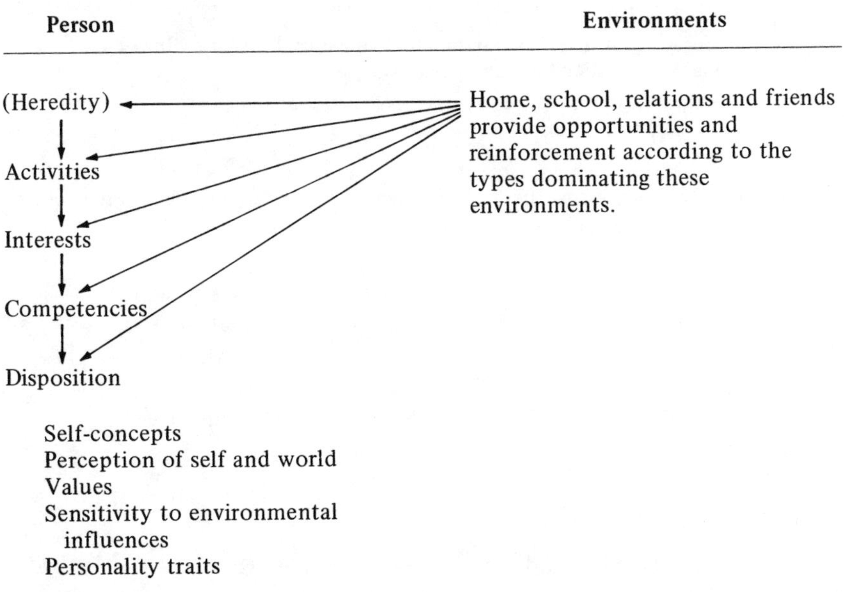

Person	Environments

(Heredity)   Home, school, relations and friends

Activities   provide opportunities and

Interests   reinforcement according to the types dominating these

Competencies   environments.

Disposition

  Self-concepts
  Perception of self and world
  Values
  Sensitivity to environmental
   influences
  Personality traits

Note: The order of development is from activities to dispositions. Preferred activities develop out of the initial global and diffuse activity that characterizes infants. We also assume that differences in heredity affect the choice of activity and the likelihood of reinforcement. For example, sheer size, sex, coordination, etc., influence the choice of sport, role in that sport, etc.

to a special disposition and how that disposition leads to a wide range of human behavior; and (3) to provide theoretical models that will fit both the old and the new evidence about the types.

The Realistic Type

The special heredity and experiences of the realistic person lead to a preference for activities that entail the explicit, ordered, or systematic manipulation of objects, tools, machines, animals, and to an aversion to educational or therapeutic activities. These behavioral tendencies lead in turn to the acquisition of manual, mechanical, agricultural, electrical, and technical competencies and to a deficit in social and educational competencies.

This development of a realistic pattern of activities, competencies, and interests creates a person who is predisposed to exhibit the following behavior:

1. He prefers realistic occupations or situations (for example, craftsman) in which he can engage in preferred activities and avoid the activities demanded by social occupations or situations.
2. He uses realistic competencies to solve problems at work and in other settings.
3. He perceives himself as having mechanical and athletic ability and lacking ability in human relations.
4. He values concrete things or tangible personal characteristics—money, power, status.

Because he possesses these preferences, competencies, self-perceptions, and values, the realistic person is apt to show himself to be:

Asocial (shy)	Materialistic	Self-effacing
Conforming	Natural	Stable
Frank	Normal	Thrifty
Genuine	Persistent	Uninsightful
Masculine	Practical	Uninvolved

The Investigative Type

The special heredity and experiences of the investigative person lead to a preference for activities that entail the observational, symbolic, systematic, and creative investigation of physical, biological, and cultural phenomena in order to understand and control such phenomena; and to an aversion to persuasive, social, and repetitive activities. These behavioral tendencies lead in turn to an acquisition of scientific and mathematical competencies and to a deficit in persuasive competencies.

This development of an investigative pattern of activities, competencies, and interests creates a person who is predisposed to exhibit the following behavior:

1. He prefers investigative occupations or situations in which he can engage in his preferred activities and competencies and avoid the activities demanded by enterprising occupations or situations.
2. He uses investigative competencies to solve problems at work and in other settings.
3. He perceives himself as scholarly, intellectually self-confident, having mathematical and scientific ability, and lacking in leadership ability.
4. He values science.

Because he possesses these preferences, competencies, self-perceptions, and values, the investigative person is apt to show himself to be:

Analytical	Introspective	Rational
Cautious	Introverted	Reserved
Critical	Methodical	Unassuming
Curious	Passive	Unpopular
Independent	Pessimistic	
Intellectual	Precise	

The Artistic Type

The special heredity and experience of the artistic person lead to a preference for ambiguous, free, unsystematized activities that entail the manipulation of physical, verbal, or human materials to create art forms or products, and to an aversion to explicit, systematic, and ordered activities. These behavioral tendencies lead, in turn, to an acquisition of artistic competencies—language, art, music, drama, writing—and to a deficit in clerical or business system competencies.

This development of an artistic pattern of activities, competencies, and interests creates a person who is predisposed to exhibit the following behavior:

1. He prefers artistic occupations or situations in which he can engage in preferred activities and competencies and avoid the activities demanded by conventional occupations or situations.
2. He uses artistic competencies to solve problems at work and in other settings.
3. He perceives himself as expressive, original, intuitive, feminine, nonconforming, introspective, independent, disorderly, having artistic and musical ability (acting, writing, speaking).
4. He values esthetic qualities.

Because he possesses these preferences, competencies, self-perceptions, and values, the artistic person is apt to show himself to be:

Complicated	Imaginative	Intuitive
Disorderly	Impractical	Nonconforming
Emotional	Impulsive	Original
Feminine	Independent	
Idealistic	Introspective	

The Social Type

The special heredity and experiences of the social person lead to a preference for activities that entail the manipulation of others to inform, train, develop, cure, or enlighten; and an aversion to explicit, ordered, systematic activities involving materials, tools, or machines. These behavioral tendencies lead in turn to an acquisition of human relations competencies such as interpersonal and educational competencies and to a deficit in manual and technical competencies.

This development of a social pattern of activities, competencies, and interests creates a person who is predisposed to exhibit the following behavior:

1. He prefers social occupations and situations in which he can engage in his preferred activities and competencies and avoid the activities demanded by realistic occupations and situations.
2. He uses social competencies to solve problems at work and in other settings.
3. He perceives himself as liking to help others, understanding of others, having teaching ability, and lacking mechanical and scientific ability.
4. He values social and ethical activities and problems.

Because he possesses these preferences, competencies, self-perceptions, and values, the social person is apt to show himself to be:

Ascendant	Helpful	Responsible
Cooperative	Idealistic	Sociable
Feminine	Insightful	Tactful
Friendly	Kind	Understanding
Generous	Persuasive	

The Enterprising Type

The special heredity and experiences of the enterprising person lead to a preference for activities that entail the manipulation of others to attain organizational goals or economic gain; and an aversion to observational, symbolic, and systematic activities. These behavioral tendencies lead in turn to an acquisition of leadership, interpersonal, and persuasive competencies, and to a deficit in scientific competencies.

This development of an enterprising pattern of activities, competencies, and interests creates a person who is predisposed to exhibit the following behavior:

1. He prefers enterprising occupations or situations in which he can engage in his preferred activities and avoid the activities demanded by investigative occupations or situations.
2. He uses enterprising competencies to solve problems at work and in other situations.
3. He perceives himself as aggressive, popular, self-confident, sociable, possessing leadership and speaking abilities, and lacking scientific ability.
4. He values political and economic achievement.

Because he possesses these preferences, competencies, self-perceptions, and values, the enterprising person is apt to show himself to be:

Acquisitive	Domineering	Optimistic
Adventurous	Energetic	Pleasure-seeking
Ambitious	Exhibitionistic	Self-confident
Argumentative	Flirtatious	Sociable
Dependent	Impulsive	Talkative

The Conventional Type

The special heredity and experiences of the conventional person lead to a preference for activities that entail the explicit, ordered, systematic manipulation of data, such as keeping records, filing materials, reproducing materials, organizing written and numerical data according to a prescribed plan, operating business machines and data processing machines to attain organizational or economic goals; and to an aversion to ambiguous, free, exploratory, or unsystematized activities. These behavioral tendencies lead in turn to an acquisition of clerical, computational, and business system competencies and to a deficit in artistic competencies.

This development of a conventional pattern of activities, competencies, and interests creates a person who is predisposed to exhibit the following behavior:

1. He prefers conventional occupations or situations in which he can engage in his preferred activities and avoid the activities demanded by artistic occupations or situations.

2. He uses conventional competencies to solve problems at work
   and in other situations.
3. He perceives himself as conforming, orderly, and as having
   clerical and numerical ability.
4. He values business and economic achievement.

Because he possesses these preferences, competencies, self-perceptions, and
values, the conventional person is apt to show himself to be:

Conforming	Inhibited	Prudish
Conscientious	Obedient	Self-controlled (calm)
Defensive	Orderly	Unimaginative
Efficient	Persistent	
Inflexible	Practical	

ASSESSMENT OF TYPES

The types have been given empirical definitions so that the validity of their
formulations can be examined and so that the typology can be applied to
everyday problems. Several related methods have been used to assess a person's
resemblance to the types.

We can assess a person's personality type by *qualitative* methods. A person
may express vocational preferences for or hold employment in an occupation
that is characteristic of a type; he may express preferences for or be engaged in
educational training that is characteristic of a type. For example, he may want
to become a physicist, or be employed as a physicist, or plan to major in physics,
or be enrolled as a physics major. Any one of these four kinds of information
results in his being classified as an investigative type. This classification is
accomplished by comparing his educational or vocational interests with
vocations assumed to be typical of each personality type (see Appendix B). In
the preceding example, "physicist" is one of the occupations that define the
investigative type. To take another example, a social worker would be classified
as a social type because "social worker" is one of the vocational criteria of this
type.

Various *quantitative* methods have also been used to assess a person's
resemblance to the types. The realistic, intellectual, social, conventional,
enterprising, and artistic scales of the Vocational Preference Inventory (Holland,
1965) provide a simple procedure for typing a person. First, the subject indicates
the vocations that appeal to him and those that do not from a list of 84
occupational titles (14 occupations for each of the six scales). The six scales are
scored and profiled. The higher a person's score on a scale, the greater his
resemblance to the type that scale represents. His highest score represents his

personality *type*; his profile of scores (obtained by ranking the scale scores from highest to lowest) represents his personality *pattern*.

The Self-directed Search (Holland, 1970, 1971a, 1971b), a vocational guidance device explicitly derived from the theory and the correlates of the Vocational Preference Inventory, appears to be another useful way to determine a person's resemblances to the types. The SDS uses a broad range of content—activities, competencies, occupations, and self-ratings—to assess the person's resemblance to each type. At this point, the SDS needs more use before its value as a defining device can be clearly ascertained, although in principle it appears to be the best psychometric technique for this purpose. The subscales of the SDS can be used to define many of the undefined terms in the formulations of the types. For example, realistic activities, competencies, self-concepts, and occupations correspond to the realistic activity, competency, self-rating, and occupation scales of the SDS, and so on (the SDS is shown in Appendix C).

The Strong Vocational Interest Blank (Strong, 1943; Campbell, 1971) has been used to assess a person's resemblance to each type (Holland, 1963) by selecting six Strong scales to represent each of the types (see Table 1). And Campbell and Holland (1972) have created six special scales from the items in the SVIB to approximate the six scales of the VPI. This alternate form of the VPI provides another way to define a person's type and personality pattern. In principle, the Kuder Preference Record (Kuder, 1960) and other interest inventories can also be used for this purpose. In short, a person's resemblance to each type may be defined by his vocational interest as manifested in his vocational and educational preferences, his current employment, or his scores on certain interest scales. The different definitions for a given type in Table 1 are assumed to be positively intercorrelated or measures of the same type, since different methods of assessment have usually produced similar results.

Although there seems to be no one best method to assess a person's personality type, the Vocational Preference Inventory, the Self-directed Search, and the use of current preference or occupation have either produced more coherent results or have special advantages by virtue of their simplicity or theoretical construction. The VPI, for example, has been extensively studied for this purpose. Because the scales are composed entirely of occupational titles, they make it easy to coordinate all other definitions of the types. The lists of occupations defining the types (actually the scales of the VPI) were used not only to designate various educational and vocational devices as being characteristic of a type, but also to indicate the vocational interest inventory scales that should be used to assess resemblance to a type. For instance, the Aviator Scale of the Strong Vocational Interest Blank was used as a measure of the realistic type, because "aviator" is among the occupations comprising the list of realistic occupations. And more recently, the VPI scales were used to create a more comprehensive occupational classification (Holland, 1966a; Holland,

TABLE 1
Personality Types and Their Definitions

	Personality Types					
Definition	*Realistic*	*Investigative*	*Artistic*	*Social*	*Enterprising*	*Conventional*
Self-directed Search	Realistic	Investigative	Artistic	Social	Enterprising	Conventional
Vocational Preference Inventory scale scores	Realistic	Intellectual	Artistic	Social	Enterprising	Conventional
Holland scales for Strong	Realistic	Investigative	Artistic	Social	Enterprising	Conventional
Kuder Preference Record scales	Outdoor Mechanical	Scientific	Artistic Musical Literary	Social service	Persuasive	Computational Clerical
Choice of major field*	Engineering Agriculture	Physics Math	Art Music	Education Social science	Business administration Political scientist	Accounting Economics
Choice of vocation*	Surveyor Mechanic	Chemist Physicist	Artist Writer	Teacher Vocational counselor	Salesman Executive	Accountant Clerk
Current occupation or work history						

*See Appendix B for more complete list of the occupations defining each type.
Note: For example, persons with high scores on any of the following scales are assumed to resemble the realistic personality type: Realistic scale (Vocational Preference Inventory); realistic scale (Strong Vocational Interest Blank); outdoor and mechanical scales (Kuder Preference Record); realistic scale (SDS); choices of major fields such as agriculture and engineering and of occupations such as mechanic, farmer, or engineer.

Viernstein, Kuo, Karweit, and Blum, 1972). The SDS can also be used to classify occupations, since it assesses the same concepts or types.

Defining types according to a person's vocational preferences or present occupation has also proved useful, because these definitions yield the most substantial predictions (Holland and Lutz, 1968; Holland and Whitney, 1968; Frantz and Walsh, 1972). However, these methods lack the flexibility provided by the VPI or the SDS. For instance, a new occupation can be classified by administering the SDS or VPI to representative samples of people employed in the new occupation. Their average scores can then be profiled and coded to indicate that occupation's specific category in the classification. At this time, no one assessment technique stands out as being the most advantageous for all purposes. It seems strategically valuable to continue to use several methods.

SUBTYPES OR PERSONALITY PATTERNS

A person's personality pattern is his profile of resemblances to the personality types. *Subtype* is a name for a particular personality pattern. Personality patterns and subtypes may consist of two to six variables or types. The number of variables used is a matter of convenience, number of subjects, and judgment. Table 2 illustrates how the six scales of the Vocational Preference Inventory or the Self-directed Search define a person's personality pattern and how that pattern is coded for research or clinical use. A person's personality pattern can also be obtained directly by noting the three-letter code associated with his current occupation (see Chapter 5 and Appendix B).

A personality pattern may be psychologically *consistent* or *inconsistent*. The pattern is consistent if its related elements have common characteristics. For example, a pattern such as realistic-investigative has many traits in common—unsociability, an orientation toward things rather than people, self-deprecation,

TABLE 2

The Coding of Interest Inventory Scales for the Study of Types and Subtypes*

Subject	Realistic	Investigative	Artistic	Social	Enterprising	Conventional	Personality Pattern
A	4	2	8	13	14	12	ESC
B	9	12	2	3	6	5	IRE
C	1	4	10	7	6	2	ASE

*Vocational Preference Inventory scale scores.
Note: The coding of profiles can be elaborated by coding all scales and by indicating the elevation of various scales, but these elaborations require extremely large samples for empirical study. For this example, we have coded each subject by his three highest scores on the VPI.

TABLE 3
Levels of Consistency

Level of Consistency	Personality Patterns
High	RI, RC, IR, IA, AI, AS, SA, SE, ES, EC, CE, CR
Middle	RA, RE, IS, IC, AR, AE, SI, SC, EA, ER, CS, CI
Low	RS, IE, AC, SR, EI, CA

and masculinity. However, a pattern such as conventional-artistic is inconsistent because it entails such oppositions as conformity and originality, control and expressiveness, and business and art. Table 3 shows three levels of consistency for all permutations and combinations of a two-variable pattern.

The *differentiation* of a personality pattern is expressed as a numerical value that equals the absolute difference between a person's highest and lowest VPI scores for the realistic, intellectual, social, conventional, enterprising, and artistic scales. These scale scores can range from 0 to 14. Well-differentiated patterns have sharp peaks and low valleys, whereas poorly differentiated patterns are relatively flat. Figure 2 illustrates how differentiation is plotted.

Although differentiation is done by an explicit and simple technique, it is a complex concept. My purpose was to create a concept that would capture what clinicians mean by a well-defined profile. To some degree, a differentiated profile will resemble a consistent profile, but differentiation is concerned more

FIGURE 2
Identical Personality Patterns with Different Degrees of Differentiation

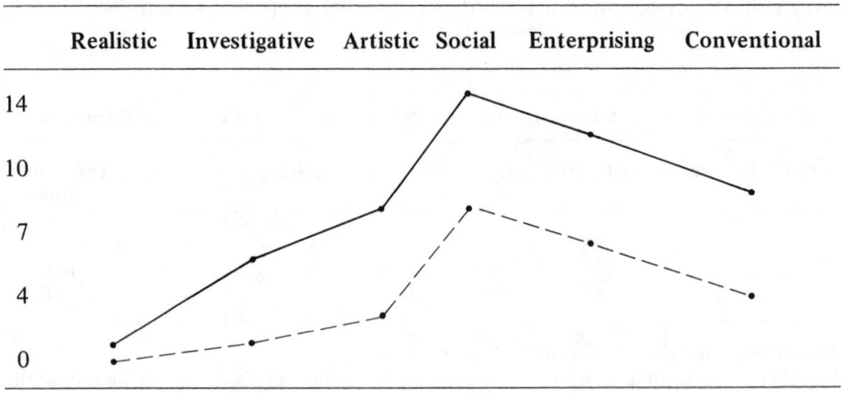

Realistic	Investigative	Artistic	Social	Enterprising	Conventional

Key: ——— equals IASECR; differentiation = 13.
        – – – equals IASECR; differentiation = 8.

with the range of scores in the whole profile than with the consistency of the highest scores.

In the extreme case, a differentiated personality pattern would represent a person who resembles a single type and no other. The opposite case would be a person with a flat profile, or a person who resembles each type to the same degree. In the first example, the person would be unusually predictable; in the second example, the person would be very unpredictable—so much so that he would be characterized more by his unpredictability than any other trait.

RELATIONSHIPS AMONG TYPES

The relationships among types, or the psychological resemblances among types, are assumed to be inversely proportional to the distances among types shown in Figure 3. The shorter the distance between any two types, the greater their similarity or psychological resemblance. For example, realistic and investigative are close together in Figure 3; therefore, they resemble one another. In contrast, investigative and enterprising types are far apart; therefore, they are

FIGURE 3

A Hexagonal Model for Defining the Psychological Resemblances Among Types and Environments and Their Interactions

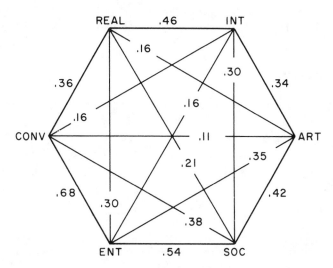

Source: Holland, J.L., Whitney, D.R., Cole, N.S., and Richards, J.M., Jr. An empirical occupational classification derived from a theory of personality and intended for practice and research. ACT Research Report No. 29. Iowa City: The American College Testing Program, 1969.

very different. Investigative and social types are at an intermediate degree of resemblance.

The hexagonal model serves three purposes in the theory: (1) It defines the degree of consistency in a person's personality pattern. Using a person's VPI profile, the two highest scale scores can be labeled as having one of three levels of consistency. Profile patterns composed of adjacent types on the hexagon are most consistent (for example, realistic-investigative, investigative-artistic, and so on). Profile patterns composed of opposite types on the hexagon are least consistent (realistic-social, investigative-enterprising, and artistic-conventional). And profile patterns composed of every other type on the hexagon form an intermediate level of consistency (for example, realistic-artistic, investigative-social, artistic-enterprising, and so on—see Table 3). (2) The hexagon defines the consistency of an environment in the same way. In this case, the percentage of types (real people) in each of the six categories is used to form an environmental profile. (3) The hexagon defines degrees of congruence between a person and his environment. The most congruent situation for a social person would be to be in a social environment. The most *in*congruent situation for a social person would be to be in a realistic environment. By using the hexagon, several intermediate degrees of congruence can be defined.

The hexagonal model, then, provides a calculus for the theory, an abstract model for linking the main ideas so that the theory can be applied to practical or theoretical problems. For instance, after the user assesses a person's type and his environment, the hexagon can be used in conjunction with the formulations for the types and environments to define degrees of consistency and congruence and to predict the expected outcomes—satisfaction, achievement, change in jobs.

TYPES AND EXPECTED PERFORMANCE

The formulations for the types imply a number of hypotheses as logical consequences. A person's resemblances to the types should predict a large portion of his behavior. The following sections summarize the major hypotheses about behavior that appear to follow from the formulations. These hypotheses are expanded and examined in Chapter 4.

Vocational Behavior

1. A person's personality type determines the primary direction of his vocational choice. Primary direction equals the choice of one of the six main groups of occupations in the classification (see Appendix B). Example: A person with an enterprising personality type will choose an enterprising occupation.
2. The types that the person resembles secondarily and tertiarily determine the secondary and tertiary directions of his

vocational choice. Here, *secondary* and *tertiary* refer to the second and third letters in a person's code, and to the second and third letters that define a particular subgroup. These concepts identify the direction of a person's choice in a more specific manner. For example, a person may aspire to social occupations, but more specifically he may aspire to subgroups of social-investigative (SI) or social-investigative-artistic (SIA).

3. Other things being equal (socio-economic status, or SES, intelligence, and so on), high vocational aspirations will be positively associated with the model types in the following order: enterprising, social, artistic, investigative, conventional, realistic.

4. The consistency of a personality pattern affects the choice of satisfying vocations and nonvocational activities. Consistency and satisfaction will be positively correlated.

5. Consistency of personality pattern affects stability of vocational choice. Consistency and stability will be positively correlated.

6. The stability of a person's work history and his tenure follow the same formulas given in hypothesis 5.

7. Consistency of personality pattern makes for effective vocational functioning or achievement.

8. Differentiation of personality pattern makes for effective vocational functioning or achievement.

9. Differentiation of personality pattern affects stability of vocational choice. Differentiation and stability will be positively correlated.

10. Other things being equal, vocational achievement will be positively associated with the model types in the following order: enterprising, social, artistic, investigative, conventional, realistic.

11. The likelihood of creative performance increases the more a personality pattern resembles the following order from high to low: artistic, investigative, social, enterprising, realistic, and conventional.

12. The specific nature of a person's occupational performance (what he does well) comes from his personality pattern. Or, the personality pattern will predict his characteristic performance or work style.

13. Competence in interpersonal relations goes with the following personality pattern order: social, enterprising, artistic, investigative, conventional, realistic. The closer a person's resemblance to this pattern order, the greater his competence.

Educational Behavior

14. The choice of, stability in, satisfaction with, and achievement in field of study follow the same rules outlined for vocational behavior.

15. Other things being equal (SES, intelligence, and so on), high educational *aspirations* go with the following personality pattern order: investigative, social, artistic, conventional, enterprising, and realistic.
16. Educational *achievement* follows the same order: investigative, social, artistic, conventional, enterprising, and realistic.
17. Persons with different personality patterns respond to instructors, teaching methods, and styles according to the formulations for the types (see formulations for personality types for specific hypotheses).

Social Behavior

18. Personality pattern determines a person's participation and leadership in social affairs. The social and enterprising types will participate more than other types.
19. Personality pattern determines a person's choice of nonvocational activities and recreations (see formulations of types).
20. Personality pattern determines a person's orientation and responsiveness to others (see formulations of types).

Environmental Responsiveness

21. Persons with consistent and differentiated personality patterns are more resistant to external influence than persons with inconsistent and undifferentiated personality patterns.
22. A person's characteristic reaction to environmental stresses is predictable from his personality pattern. The various types will be expected to cope with stress in the same way that they cope with everyday problems (see formulations of types).

SUMMARY

The formulations for the types are models for assessing people, for discovering how they may have grown up, how they can be identified, how they can be expected to perceive and behave, and how types are related to one another. The personality types are also models for organizing knowledge, conceptualizing personality, developing practical applications, and stimulating research.

The Environmental Models

chapter 3

Because human behavior depends upon both personality *and* the environment in which a person lives, the personality types must be supplemented by environmental information. To accomplish this task, six model environments have been proposed to characterize the common social and physical environments in our culture. The model environments correspond to the personality types.

Just as we can assess real people by comparing them with the personality types, we can assess real environments by comparing them with the models—that is, with the descriptions of hypothetical environments. The personality type reflects vocational preferences. An environmental model may be defined as the situation or atmosphere created by the people who dominate a given environment. For instance, a social environment would be an environment dominated by social types.

Because the personality types and the environmental models share a common set of constructs, it is possible to classify people and environments in the same terms and thus to predict the outcome of pairing people and environments. More explicitly, we can predict what will happen when a particular person is put into a particular environment by characterizing the person and his environment in terms of the types and models and reviewing the appropriate formulations in order to discover the congruities and incongruities the models suggest. For example, the interaction of a conventional type and a conventional environment should produce a number of desirable outcomes, such as work satisfaction, achievement, and vocational stability. This chapter and the next provide a complete account of the explanatory values of the theory for these purposes. The typology gives us a tremendous advantage both in planning research and in interpreting results. Without it, we would have to deal with a formidable number of possible person-environment interactions; with it, we have relatively few variables to juggle and an explicit rationale to guide us.

DEVELOPMENT OF MODELS

The construction of the model environments rests mainly on the suggestion made by Linton (1945) and others that most of our environment is transmitted through other people. This implies that the character of an environment reflects the nature of its members and that the dominant features of an environment reflect the typical characteristics of its members. If we know what kind of people make up a group, we can infer the climate that the group creates. For example, an office full of engineers would be expected to have a different atmosphere from that of an office full of accountants. An informal gathering of salesmen would differ in atmosphere from an informal gathering of ministers.

The formula—types flourish in congruent environments—needs many qualifications about the environment and the position of the person in the environment in order to be successfully applied. First, environments rarely have a homogeneous character, so where a person is located in a particular environment will determine the kind and amount of stimulation he will receive. For instance, students attending different classes in the same school or college undergo different experiences; employees working in different departments of a large organization undergo different experiences; students attending the same college but living at home or in dorms are subject to different experiences. It is therefore important to assess the subenvironmental unit that makes up the largest or most influential portion of a person's environment. Second, it is equally important to estimate the psychological field or the environment that a person perceives as his. The weak impact of many educational and work environments occurs because a person is attending more to friends, family, or colleagues who may be remote from his immediate physical environment. Third, the institutional demands of jobs, schools, or churches must be distinguished from the influences of the people who populate these institutions. Institutional influences such as job descriptions and rules and regulations may exert one kind of influence, but the network of personal relationships may exert another kind. Fourth, because power over others is not usually distributed evenly, it seems important to assess what types have the most power. For instance, in a small, family-owned business, a father and son (according to type) may create a distinct and influential environment so that other types in the environment have only minor influence. Finally, the size and complexity of an environment—especially size—appear to have influences that are often independent of the distribution of types or other forces.

At this point, there is no simple or clear resolution of these practical and theoretical difficulties. At the same time, this summary of the complexities involved in describing the environment and how persons and environments interact suggests some useful courses of action for practice and research. They include the following: (1) Estimate the time spent in an environment. (2) Check to see if the person is in a special subunit that can be isolated and assessed. (3) Characterize the distribution of power and determine whether power should be taken into consideration. (4) Ascertain the person's perception of his environment. (5) Control for size of environment or organization if at all possible. In short, examine and control for the influences that a simple census of types in an environment cannot hope to deal with.

FORMULATIONS

The descriptions of the model environments parallel the formulations for the personality types: Both kinds of formulations focus on activities, competencies, perceptions, and values.

The Realistic Environment

The realistic environment is characterized by the dominance of environmental demands and opportunities that entail the explicit, ordered, or systematic manipulation of objects, tools, machines, and animals, and by a population dominated by realistic types. These demands, opportunities, and realistic people create a characteristic atmosphere that operates in the following way:

1. It stimulates people to perform realistic activities such as using machines and tools.
2. It fosters technical competencies and achievements.
3. It encourages people to see themselves as having mechanical ability and lacking ability in human relations; it encourages them to see the world in simple, tangible, and traditional terms.
4. It rewards people for the display of conventional values and goods: money, power, and possessions.

These environmental experiences lead to secondary effects. People become:

1. More susceptible to pragmatic, masculine, and conventional influences.
2. More attracted to realistic occupations and roles in which they can express themselves in realistic activities.
3. Less adept at coping with others; they learn instead simple, direct, masculine coping methods.

People acquire, or are reinforced in, these traits—they are:

Conforming	Normal	Stable
Frank	Persistent	Thrifty
Genuine	Practical	Uninsightful

Masculine	Self-effacing	Uninvolved
Materialistic	Shy	

The Investigative Environment

The investigative environment is characterized by the dominance of environmental demands and opportunities that entail the observation and symbolic, systematic, creative investigation of physical, biological, or cultural phenomena, and by a population dominated by investigative types. These demands, opportunities, and investigative people create a characteristic atmosphere that operates to produce the following outcomes:

1. It stimulates people to perform investigative activities.
2. It encourages scientific competencies and achievements.
3. It encourages people to see themselves as scholarly, as having mathematical and scientific ability, and as lacking in leadership ability; it encourages them to see the world in complex, abstract, independent, and original ways.
4. It rewards people for the display of scientific values.

These environmental experiences lead to secondary effects. People become:

1. More susceptible to abstract, theoretical, and analytic influences.
2. More attracted to investigative occupations and roles in which they can express themselves in investigative activities.
3. More apt to cope with others in rational, analytic, and indirect ways.

People acquire, or are reinforced in, these traits—they are:

Analytical	Introspective	Rational
Cautious	Introverted	Reserved
Critical	Methodical	Unassuming
Curious	Passive	Unpopular
Independent	Pessimistic	
Intellectual	Precise	

The Artistic Environment

The artistic environment is characterized by the dominance of environmental demands and opportunities that entail ambiguous, free, unsystematized activities and competencies to create art forms or products, and by the dominance of artistic types in the environment. These demands, opportunities, and artistic people create a characteristic atmosphere that operates to produce the following outcomes:

1. It stimulates people to engage in artistic activities.
2. It fosters artistic competencies and achievements.
3. It encourages people to see themselves as expressive, original, intuitive, feminine, nonconforming, independent, and as having artistic abilities (acting, writing, speaking). It encourages people to see the world in complex, independent, unconventional, and flexible ways.
4. It rewards people for the display of artistic values.

These environmental experiences lead to secondary effects. People become:

1. More susceptible to personal, emotional, and imaginative influences.
2. More attracted to artistic occupations and roles in which they can express themselves in artistic activities.
3. More likely to cope with others in personal, emotional, expressive, and unconventional ways.

People acquire, or are reinforced in, these traits—they are:

Complicated	Imaginative	Intuitive
Disorderly	Impractical	Nonconforming
Emotional	Impulsive	Original
Feminine	Independent	
Idealistic	Introspective	

The Social Environment

The social environment is characterized by the dominance of environmental demands and opportunities that entail the manipulation of others to inform, train, develop, cure, or enlighten, and by a population dominated by social types. These demands, opportunities, and social people create a characteristic atmosphere that operates to produce the following goals and outcomes:

1. It stimulates people to engage in social activities.
2. It fosters social competencies.
3. It encourages people to see themselves as liking to help others, understanding of others, cooperative, and sociable; it encourages them to see the world in flexible ways.
4. It rewards people for the display of social values.

These environmental forces lead to secondary effects. People become:

1. More susceptible to social, humanitarian, and religious influences.
2. More attracted to social occupations and roles in which they can express themselves in social activities.

3. More apt to cope with others by being friendly, helpful, cooperative.

People acquire, or are reinforced in, these traits—they are:

Ascendant	Helpful	Responsible
Cooperative	Idealistic	Sociable
Feminine	Insightful	Tactful
Friendly	Kind	Understanding
Generous	Persuasive	

The Enterprising Environment

The enterprising environment is characterized by the dominance of environmental demands and opportunities that entail the manipulation of others to attain organizational or self-interest goals, and by the dominance of enterprising types. These demands, opportunities, and enterprising people create a characteristic atmosphere that operates to produce the following goals and outcomes:

1. It stimulates people to engage in enterprising activities, such as selling, or leading others.
2. It fosters enterprising competencies and achievements.
3. It encourages people to see themselves as aggressive, popular, self-confident, sociable, and as possessing leadership and speaking ability. It encourages people to see the world in terms of power, status, responsibility, and in stereotyped, constricted, dependent, and simple terms.
4. It rewards people for the display of enterprising values and goals: money, power, and status.

These environmental experiences lead to secondary effects. People become:

1. More susceptible to social, emotional, and materialistic influences.
2. More attracted to enterprising occupations and roles in which they can express themselves in enterprising activities.
3. More prone to cope with others in an enterprising manner—by dominance, talkativeness, and so on.

People acquire, or are reinforced in, these traits—they are:

Acquisitive	Dependent	Impulsive
Adventurous	Energetic	Pleasure-seeking
Ambitious	Exhibitionistic	Self-confident
Argumentative	Flirtatious	Sociable

The Conventional Environment

The conventional environment is characterized by the dominance of environmental demands and opportunities that entail the explicit, ordered, systematic manipulation of data, such as keeping records, filing materials, reproducing materials, organizing written and numerical data according to a prescribed plan, operating business and data processing machines, and by a population dominated by conventional types. These demands, opportunities, and conventional people create a characteristic atmosphere that operates to produce the following goals and outcomes:

1. It stimulates people to engage in conventional activities, such as recording and organizing data or records.
2. It fosters conventional competencies and achievements.
3. It encourages people to see themselves as conforming, orderly, nonartistic, and as having clerical competencies; it encourages them to see the world in conventional, stereotyped, constricted, simple, dependent ways.
4. It rewards people for the display of conventional values: money, dependability, conformity.

These environmental experiences lead to secondary effects. People become:

1. More susceptible to materialistic influences: money, position, power.
2. More attracted to conventional occupations and roles.
3. More prone to cope with others in a conventional manner—to be controlling, conforming, practical.

People acquire, or are reinforced in, these traits—they are:

Conforming	Inhibited	Prudish
Conscientious	Obedient	Self-controlled
Defensive	Orderly	Unimaginative
Efficient	Persistent	
Inflexible	Practical	

DEFINING THE ENVIRONMENT

Because many of the psychologically important features of the environment consist of or are transmitted by the people in it, we can characterize an environment by assessing its population. The Environmental Assessment Technique (EAT) was developed for this purpose, and it can be used to assess the population of a college, a hospital, a business, a community, or of any other institution or group. The technique entails taking a census of the occupations, training preferences, or vocational preferences of a population. These preferences or occupations are categorized according to the criteria for class membership as belonging to one of the six environments. This classification results in a six-variable profile. The absolute numbers for each type are then converted to percentages of the total population for the particular environment or institution.

For example, a business with two hundred employees might have the distribution of types shown in Table 4. The environmental pattern of this business would be represented by the code CERSIA, because the dominant type in this environment is the conventional, followed by the enterprising, and so on. Such an environment would be expected to emphasize, among other factors, orderliness, social status, and conservative economic and political beliefs. Similar codes can be obtained for colleges by a census and categorization of the proportion of students in different major fields, or for neighborhoods by a census of the occupations of households.

The *consistency* of an environmental pattern is defined by the same patterns and relationships given in Table 3 and Figure 3. Consistent environments provide similar rewards and demands; inconsistent environments provide divergent rewards and demands.

The *differentiation* of an environment is also defined following the same principle given for defining the differentiation of a personality pattern. In this case, the percentage difference between the most and least common personality types in a given environment equals the degree of differentiation of that environment. In the example in Table 4, the differentiation is 64 minus 2 or 62.

Differentiated environments encourage a narrow range of behavior in explicit ways; undifferentiated environments stimulate a broad range of behavior and provide ambiguous guidance. The differentiated environment is analogous to the person who resembles only one personality type; the undifferentiated environment is analogous to the person with a flat profile who resembles each type to the same degree.

TABLE 4

The Environmental Assessment Technique

Type	Number	Percentage
Realistic	20	10%
Investigative	8	4
Social	12	6
Conventional	128	64
Enterprising	28	14
Artistic	4	2
Total	200	100%

INTERNAL RELATIONSHIPS

The relationships among the six kinds of environmental models are defined by the hexagonal model given earlier (Figure 3). The closer two environmental models are in the hexagon, the greater the similarity. The farther apart they are, the more divergent are their reinforcing properties. The consistency of environments is a simple method for describing the relationships between environments taken two at a time. The more general formula provided by the use of the hexagon makes it possible to describe the relationships of the six model environments within a single natural environment or the relationships between two natural environments that may impinge on one another: one company versus another, one neighborhood versus another, one school versus another.

EXPECTED INFLUENCES

Like the personality types, the model environments imply many hypotheses about a person's vocational, personal, educational, and social behavior. The following hypotheses are derived from the model formulations; they are regarded simply as axiomatic statements from which some inferences can be drawn.

Vocational Behavior

1. Each model environment attracts its associated personality type. Realistic environments attract realistic types; investigative environments attract investigative types, and so on. Also, each environment repels some types more than others (see Figure 3).
2. The degree of influence that an environment exerts for vocational stability (number of job changes per unit of time and the psychological distances of such changes) follows this descending order: R, C, E, S, A, I.
3. Consistency of the environmental pattern promotes stability of vocational choice—affects the number and degrees of change.
4. Differentiation of an environment promotes stability of vocational choice.
5. Each model environment reinforces its own characteristic achievement. The realistic environment promotes realistic achievement; the investigative environment promotes investigative achievement, and so on.
6. The consistency and differentiation of an environment interact to increase both the stability and the level of vocational achievement.

7. The consistency of an environment promotes vocational satisfaction and the differentiation of an environment promotes vocational satisfaction.

8. Other things being equal (income and training), the explicitness of an environment promotes vocational satisfaction. The environments in descending order of explicitness are: C, R, I, E, S, A.

Personal Effectiveness

9. The model environments promote creative performance in the following descending order: A, I, S, E, R, C.

10. Each model environment reinforces a characteristic group of activities, competencies, and predispositions.

11. Consistent environments promote effective performance.

Educational Behavior

12. Each model environment reinforces a characteristic group of educational behaviors.

Social Behavior

13. Each model environment reinforces a characteristic group of social behaviors.

Sensitization

14. Each model environment sensitizes people or makes them more responsive to special stimuli such as characteristic attitudes, values, roles, and so on.

SUMMARY

The environmental models were developed to provide a more complete model for understanding human behavior. The environmental formulations are patterned after the personality types and can be applied to natural environments by categorizing the occupations or vocational interests of the inhabitants according to the classification scheme summarized in Chapter 5 and elaborated in Appendix B.

People in Environments

chapter 4

The formulations for the personality types and the model environments provide the tools to describe and comprehend what happens when a particular kind of person lives in a particular environment.

The implications of the formulations for person-environment interactions have been divided into two main topics: (1) definitions and processes in person-environment interactions and (2) applications of the definitions and formulations to vocational life, personal effectiveness, educational behavior, social behavior, and environmental responsiveness.

DEFINITIONS AND PROCESSES

The following paragraphs define and illustrate three methods for characterizing the pairing of a person and his environment. Like the definitions of the types and environments, the definitions of interactions are needed to apply the theory to practical problems.

Degrees of Congruence

A person's relationship to his environment can be assessed according to the degree of congruence or compatibility. This assessment is defined by the hexagonal model. The most extreme degree of congruence is the situation in which a personality type is in a matching environment—for example, a realistic person in a realistic environment. The next degree of congruence is that of a personality type in an adjacent environment, such as a realistic person in an investigative or conventional environment. A realistic person in an artistic or enterprising environment represents a third and lesser degree of congruence.

Finally, the most extreme degree of incongruence is the situation in which a personality type is in an opposite environment, such as a realistic person in a social environment. By using the hexagonal model in Figure 3, four levels of congruence can be obtained for each of the six types. More levels can be derived by using two- or three-letter codes for types and environments—for example, an RI type in an RI environment, an RI type in an IR environment, an RI in an RA or RC environment, and so on.

The personal and situation characteristics that create a particular degree of congruence can be made explicit by reviewing the formulations for the type and the environment involved. For instance, a social type in a social environment is an extreme case of congruence for many reasons. The social person is provided an opportunity to engage in social activities, to use social competencies, to perform services he values, to see himself as understanding and helpful, and to exhibit personality traits of generosity, friendliness, and sociability. In turn, the social environment reinforces the self-image the social type brings to the environment and rewards him for social values and social personality traits such as generosity, friendliness, and sociability. Of perhaps equal importance, a social type in a social environment can also avoid the activities he dislikes, the demands for competencies he lacks, the tasks and self-images he does not value, and the situations in which his personality traits are not encouraged.

The content and structure of incongruent interactions can be elaborated in the same way. The formulations, then, serve to show how people and environments affect one another. For example, a conventional type in an artistic environment would discover the following kinds of oppositions or incongruities: He likes structured activities, but the environment provides unstructured activities; he possesses conventional competencies, but the environment demands artistic competencies; he looks at the world in conservative ways, but the people in the artistic environment look at the world in unconventional ways; his personal traits such as orderliness and inhibition are deprecated by artistic types who tend to be his opposite, who are disorderly and impulsive. Taken together, these negative interactions should result in gross dissatisfaction, ineffective coping behavior, and probably leaving the environment.

Degrees of Consistency

The outcomes of an interaction are influenced by the consistency of a person's personality pattern and the consistency of the environmental pattern. This assumption comes from the definitions of consistency (three levels) given earlier. For the person, a more consistent personality pattern represents an integration of similar interests, competencies, values, traits, and perceptions. Presumably such people are more predictable as well as more resistant to influence. For the environment, a more consistent pattern represents an integration of similar demands and rewards. Consequently, a more consistent environment usually exerts pressure for similar behavior.

Inconsistent persons are less predictable because they combine more diverse interests, competencies, values, and perceptions. As a result, they have a more extensive repertoire of possible behaviors. Inconsistent environments are less influential, because they provide a wide rather than a narrow range of demands and rewards. With this background, it is reasonable that the interactions of consistent persons and consistent environments will result in more predictable outcomes, and that these outcomes will influence both the persons and their environments to a greater degree.

Degrees of Differentiation

Other things being equal (congruence and consistency), interactions are also affected by the differentiation of types and environments. Differentiation means the magnitude of the difference between highest and lowest scores on the six variables used to determine a person's or an environment's degree of resemblance to a personality type or an environmental model. The greater the difference between the highest and lowest of the six scores, the greater the differentiation. Graphically, the profile of a differentiated pattern will have high peaks and low valleys; the profile of an undifferentiated pattern will appear relatively flat. Figure 2 shows two identical personality or environmental patterns that have different degrees of differentiation.

The interaction of a differentiated person and a differentiated environment will be most predictable and intense because a well-defined (predictable, and therefore understandable) person is interacting with a well-defined environment that has a focused influence. The interaction of an undifferentiated person and environment will be least predictable, because undifferentiated persons and environments are composed of diverse elements and forces and so have a diffuse influence. When the person and environment are differentiated and undifferentiated or vice-versa, the interaction falls between these two extremes of predictability and intensity. To summarize, the differentiation of the personality or environmental pattern increases both the possibility that the hypothesized behavior in the formulations will occur and the magnitude of the hypothesized behavior.

Combinations of Congruence, Consistency, and Differentiation

Interactions involving different degrees of congruence, consistency, and differentiation will result in different kinds and degrees of outcomes. At one extreme, the interaction of a type and model environment that are congruent, consistent, and differentiated will intensify and make more predictable the hypotheses about vocational life, personal effectiveness, educational behavior, social behavior, and environmental responsiveness. For example, a conventional-enterprising person whose personality pattern is consistent and differentiated and who enters a conventional-enterprising environment with a high degree of differentiation will probably do competent work, be satisfied and personally effective, and engage in appropriate social and educational behavior. At the other extreme, incongruence, inconsistency, and undifferentiation make for uncertain predictions and outcomes: unpredictable vocational behavior, dissatisfaction, and ineffective functioning.

The relative influence or importance of these characteristics seems to be as follows: Congruence of the person-environment interaction is most influential; differentiation of person or environment is next, and consistency of person or environment is least influential. Table 5 summarizes how a particular interaction can be structured and analyzed by using the formulations for types and environments. Any interaction can be examined by using this cross-sectional plan for reviewing the main forces involved.

THEORETICAL APPLICATIONS

This section applies the definitions of person-environment interactions to the phenomena of vocational, educational, and social behavior. In addition, the definitions and processes outlined earlier are used to develop a comprehensive plan for examining these phenomena and for explaining stability and change in personal behavior.

A Comprehensive Plan

The definitions of the personality types and model environments and the formulations about their interactions make it possible to trace a person's development and examine his principal environments from the time he can express a vocational preference to the time of his death. The person can be assessed by his vocational preferences at different points in his life. His

TABLE 5

The Structure of Person-Environment Interactions

Person	Environment	Outcomes
Activities ⟶	Opportunities ⟶	Interests
Competencies ⟶	Demands ⟶	Proficiency
Perceptions ⟶	Encouragement ⟶	Outlook
Self		
World		
Values ⟶	Encouragement ⟶	Values
Traits ⟶	Encouragement ⟶	Traits

environments—family background, school, work situations, and so on—can be assessed using the Environmental Assessment Technique (see page 34). By applying the theory with its classes and subclasses and relatively simple sets of definitions to an entire life span, we can use a great range of information about human behavior and environments, and thus more easily study person-environment interactions and their outcomes.

Figure 4 illustrates this comprehensive, longitudinal model for explaining a person's life history. The formulation can be elaborated in many ways: by assigning single-letter codes to the person and each environment and then, on the basis of the formulations for the personality types and the environmental models, making predictions about interactions and outcomes; or by assigning two- or three-letter codes to each type and environment in the life span. In this way, a person's movement from vocational preference to vocational preference, major field to major field, field of training to job, or job to job can be studied and interpreted in the context of the theory as vocational, educational, or social behavior.

Stability and Change

The comprehensive plan requires some supplementary formulations to cope with the problems of stability and change in human behavior: Why do

FIGURE 4
The Interactions of Persons and Environments

Time	Environment	Types
	Parents ————————————————→	Children
		↓
	Neighborhoods ————————————————→	Students
		↓
	High schools ————————————————→	Students
		↓
	Religious and other social institutions ————→	Students
		↓
	Technical schools and colleges ————→	Students
		↓
	First job ————————————————→	Adults
		↓
	Next job ————————————————→	Adults
		↓
	Last job ————————————————→	Adults

some people continue to choose the same kind of occupation; why do others move between markedly different kinds of jobs? The following hypotheses have been devised from the previous formulations and are proposed to explain the processes of stability and change.

1. A person finds his environment reinforcing and satisfying when the environmental pattern resembles his personality pattern. This situation makes for stability of behavior because the person receives a good deal of selective reinforcement of his behavior. The greater the discrepancy between a person's personality pattern and his environmental pattern, the more dissatisfying, uncomfortable, and destructive this interaction becomes. Discrepancy is assessed by the hexagonal model.

2. Friendships and therapeutic and teaching relationships depend upon the same formulation given in hypothesis 1.

3. Incongruent interactions stimulate change in human behavior; conversely, congruent interactions encourage stability of behavior. Persons tend to change or become like the dominant persons in the environment. This tendency is greater, the greater the degree of congruence between person and environment. Those persons who are most incongruent will be changed least. Or, the closer a person is to the core of an environment, the greater the influence of the environment.

4. A person resolves incongruence by seeking a new and congruent environment, by remaking his present environment, or by changing his behavior.
   A. Differentiation and consistency of personality pattern usually make for a change of environment in the face of an incongruent environment.
   B. Persons with differentiated and consistent personality patterns are more apt to remake the environment itself, if they cannot leave it, to achieve greater congruence. For example, people usually hire people whom they like or see as congenial.
   C. Persons with undifferentiated and inconsistent personality patterns tend to adapt to incongruence by changing their own behavior and personality pattern to achieve greater congruence with their environment.
   D. A person's tendency to leave an environment increases as the incongruity of the interaction increases (see hexagon, Figure 3, for degrees of congruity).

These general formulations are most applicable to vocational behavior, because that kind of experience has been the major source of stimulation and support for these ideas. At the same time, they also appear applicable to other phenomena, to educational and social behavior.

Vocational Behavior

When the main hypotheses about personality types are seen in the context of interactions with the environment, these additional hypotheses appear to follow:

1. The direction of a person's vocational choice is stabilized or maintained when he lives in a congruent environment. Conversely, the direction of a person's vocational choice tends to change when he lives in an incongruent environment. (The stability or change in a person's work history follows the same principle.)
2. The level of a person's vocational choice is stabilized by a congruent environment. Conversely, an incongruent environment tends to change a person's level of vocational aspiration.
3. The level of a person's occupational achievement is encouraged by the congruence of his work environment.
4. The degree of a person's vocational satisfaction is encouraged by the congruence of his work environment.

These hypotheses are also conditioned by the vocational maturity of a person's profile—consistency and differentiation—and his place within the environment.

Educational Behavior

The hypotheses derived from the personality types about educational behavior resemble those for vocational behavior. The choice of, stability in, satisfaction with, and achievement in a field of training or study follow the identical rules outlined for vocational behavior. In the same way, persons respond positively to instructors whose personality patterns resemble their own.

Personal Development and Effectiveness

Emotional stability is initiated in large part by a person's early experiences, particularly those of his childhood. The stable person probably has parents whose individual personality patterns are consistent both in themselves and in relation to the other parent's personality pattern. Consequently, the parents' values and child-rearing practices are harmonious and free of major conflict. These attributes foster consistent, integrated behavior in the child. Because the child perceives himself and the world accurately, he is more likely to select congruent environments for training and eventual vocation. This selection leads to achievement, reinforcement, and satisfaction.

If, however, one or both parents have inconsistent personality patterns, or if the father's pattern is incongruent with the mother's, then the child is likely to develop an inaccurate picture of himself and the world, inconsistent values, inconsistent interests and competencies, and little self-confidence. Consequently, he will tend to vacillate, to make poor choices of environments, and to function ineffectively even in compatible environments.

In short, personal stability is the outcome of passing through a series of consistent environments that strengthen one's ability to cope with the world in an integrated way. Instability, in contrast, results from living in a succession of inconsistent environments that create and perpetuate inaccurate perceptions of self and world, divergent interests and competencies, and conflicting values. The hypotheses concerned with personal effectiveness (creative performance, style of work, interpersonal competence) are all more likely to occur when the person locates or is placed in a congruent environment.

Social Behavior

The more congruent a person's environment is with his personality pattern, the more likely he will exhibit the social and avocational behaviors hypothesized from his personality pattern: (1) participation and leadership in social affairs, (2) choice and maintenance of interest in nonvocational activities and recreations, (3) interest in and responsiveness to others in his environment. In contrast, the more incongruent his environment, the greater the likelihood that the person will not participate or exhibit these behaviors.

Environmental Responsiveness

Other things being equal (consistency, differentiation, intelligence, and social status), types resist the influence of their environment the more divergent their personality pattern is from the environmental pattern. And the closer the resemblance of personality and environmental patterns, the more sensitive and pliable the person becomes.

SUMMARY

Some methods for explaining the processes in person-environment interactions have been outlined. The application of these methods to vocational, educational, and social behavior has been illustrated, and the formulations about the types and environments have been used to derive some expected outcomes.

Some Evidence

The purpose of this chapter is to summarize the evidence for the usefulness of the theory and its classification scheme. This review includes all revelant information for the period 1959 through 1971, with a few reports from 1972. In contrast to the first two reports on the theory (Holland, 1959, 1966b), this account focuses on direct evidence (experimental tests of hypotheses) rather than indirect evidence, although some related or indirect evidence has been included.

Because there are more than a hundred studies to review, only the most important are summarized in any detail. The poorer studies (those that were poorly planned and executed, with ambiguous results) will be mentioned only briefly. The studies have been grouped as follows: personality types, environmental models, interactions, classification, and new research needs.

PERSONALITY TYPES

Hypotheses about the personality types have attracted the most research interest. Using the definitions suggested in the first or second statement of the theory (Holland, 1959, 1966b) or special definitions of their own, a number of investigators have assessed elementary, high school, college, and graduate students, as well as employed adults, to test hypotheses about the types. To make the studies more amenable to summary and analysis, they have been grouped according to purpose: (1) Testing hypotheses about the characteristics of types, (2) extending the original interest measures as definitions to more remote scales or assessments, (3) testing hypotheses about the development of types, (4) testing hypotheses about the perceptions of types, and (5) examining how types search for new environments.

Characteristics

The many attempts to show whether or not the characteristics attributed to types have validity are difficult to categorize. Only a few studies use a single set of theoretical definitions and a single set of criteria, and test only concurrent or predictive relationships; most studies are elaborate mixtures of tests of concurrent and longitudinal relationships and use multiple measures to determine the characteristics of types. Because of these complexities, it seemed useful to organize the evidence according to researcher or research teams.

Most of the early studies of the types, which were done by Holland and his colleagues, are characterized by the use of multiple dependent variables and multiple methods for the definition of types. In short, these exploratory studies usually capitalized on almost any readily available data in an attempt to develop fuller knowledge. Because these shotgun studies produced a large number of analyses, only the principal findings will be summarized.

In one early study that appeared as a monograph, Holland (1962) assessed two large samples of bright high school graduates (National Merit finalists) over one- and two-year intervals (N = 1,177 and 994). Using VPI scale scores, vocational choice, or choice of major field to define a student's type, Holland found that a broad range of personal characteristics, usually bearing out the theory, was associated with the types. These included academic aptitudes, self-ratings, extracurricular activities, academic interests, nonacademic achievements, and personality variables (16 PF).

Although this first study was generally positive, it revealed two major deficiencies. The findings for a particular type often overlapped those for a similar type, and the formulations (Holland, 1959) were not sufficiently explicit or comprehensive to cope with the myriad results dredged up by this data-rich study. On the positive side, most analyses were statistically significant and were moderately efficient.

In a second monograph, Holland (1963) again used a sample of National Merit finalists (N = 592). This longitudinal study differed from the first in two ways: the time interval was longer (first to fourth year of college) and six scales of the Strong Vocational Interest Blank were selected to assess the types. Using the Strong scales and the choice of vocation and major field to define a student's resemblance to the types and a similar array of dependent variables (choice of field at graduation, self-ratings, extracurricular achievements, and so on), Holland produced findings that approximated those obtained in the first study. A similar pattern of success and failure was observed. On the one hand, the use of the Strong scales demonstrated that the types could be defined by different instruments to yield similar results. At the same time, the overlapping among types persisted in some analyses, and the deficiencies of the first set of formulations were observed again—lack of clarity and comprehensiveness.

In a third report, Holland and Nichols (1964) studied changes in major field plans for a one-year period (high school senior year to end of freshman year in college). They assessed a sample of National Merit finalists (332 boys and 181 girls) in high school with interest, personality, originality, self-rating, achievement, and aptitude measures; they then assessed the students again in college and compared their pre- and post-college plans. Remaining in a given field (classified according to the typology) appears to be related to having personal attributes commonly associated with those of the typical student; leaving a field is related to dissimilarity between a student's attributes and those of the typical student. For example, boys who left realistic fields (largely engineering in this instance) appeared to be irresponsible, original, tolerant of ambiguity, and complex in outlook. In contrast, boys who remained in realistic fields were responsible, unoriginal, intolerant of ambiguity, and simple in outlook.

These and other findings are tenuous because a much larger sample would have been necessary to produce reliable findings. Large samples are required because the categorization according to type and sex reduces the usable portion of a sample to one-twelfth of its total, and the typical sample attrition decimates these subcategories even more.

In a fourth report, Holland (1963-64) used another sample of bright students to test some hypotheses about types (360 boys and 278 girls). Students filled out a questionnaire that included items about their vocational choices, an adjective checklist, self-ratings, multiple-choice questions about how they cope with problems, and sentence stems about vocations.

The cross-sectional analyses of these data indicated that students classified as different types according to their VPI scores described themselves in expected ways. For example, boys categorized as investigative characterized themselves as analytical, curious, hard-headed, imaginative, intellectual, mechanical, not popular, quiet, reserved, scholarly, scientific, and so on. The majority of adjectives associated with the other types yielded similar positive evidence, although a few adjectives appeared either inconsistent with or unanticipated by the formulation for a given type. Similar results were obtained when types were studied for their characteristic reactions to stress, competencies in various fields, and most enjoyable activities. For example, boys with high scores on the realistic scale of the VPI said that they "most enjoy working with their hands, tools, or instruments"; that they would find it most frustrating to "take patients in mental hospitals on recreational trips"; that they believe their "greatest ability lies in the area of mechanics"; and that they are "most incompetent in the area of human relations."

The fifth report (Holland, 1964), a one-year longitudinal study like four of five earlier reports, replicated many previous findings about the characteristics of types and extended the range of personal characteristics found to be related to the types. Using a sample of 1,437 National Merit finalists, the investigator correlated VPI scores with self-ratings, life goals, and achievements. Again, student characteristics were usually associated with appropriate types. For example, boys with many social preferences (high social scale on VPI) rated themselves high on understanding of others, cooperativeness, and interest in religion.

The sixth monograph in this series (Holland, 1968b) is perhaps the most valuable, since a large sample of college freshmen from 28 colleges with a wide range of academic talent and social status was employed (1,576 men and 1,571 women). Although the sample was not a representative one, it did allow a large-scale test of the theory with a relatively normal group (in contrast to National Merit finalists).

Students were categorized as types and subtypes according to their VPI profiles and then compared on twenty-two dependent variables including competencies, life goals, self-ratings, and personality and attitudinal variables. Simple analyses of variance usually showed substantial differences across the types. Comparisons across subtypes such as RI, RS, RC, RE, and RA were also significant, and even comparisons across closely related subtypes yielded some differences—for example, RIS, RIC, RIE, and RIA.

The results of this study extended those of previous studies, with some differences: (1) The results for women were more positive than those for men. In all earlier studies, it had been the other way around. (2) The results were more explicit and substantial. A count of the theoretically expected high mean scores for types and subtypes is as follows: For men, 76 percent of the predictions are correct for comparisons across types, 75 percent are correct across two-letter subtypes, and 64.1 percent are correct across three-letter subtypes. For women, these percentages are 84.0, 75.4, and 72.7, respectively. (3) The overlapping among types remained but seemed less pronounced than before, although no statistical tests were performed. (4) These statistical tests strongly suggested that people with similar codes have similar characteristics, which means that as we move from comparisons across types to comparisons of subtypes, there will be an obvious increasing similarity of personalities. This is implied by the F tests, which decrease dramatically in size from comparisons across types to comparisons within types (see Tables 2-7, Holland, 1968b).

Abe and Holland (1965a) assessed 12,432 college freshmen in thirty-one colleges and universities for their interests, favorite activities, attitudes, life goals, and vocational aspirations. Students were classified by vocational aspiration and compared on 117 variables. In general, many comparisons resulted in large mean differences that were consistent with the formulations for the personality types. These results became especially supportive when they were classified in categories analogous to the types (see Tables 4-15, Abe and Holland, 1965a). Abe and Holland (1965b) also used a student's choice of major field as the independent variable in place of his vocational choice, and repeated the analyses just described. The results closely resembled those obtained by the use of vocational choice.

Wall, Osipow, and Ashby (1967), using a sample of 186 male college freshmen, demonstrated that a student's ranking of six descriptions of the types according to his resemblance to each resulted in relatively clear and significant relationships between student rankings and SVIB group scores. In short, students see themselves in ways that correspond with their interest scores. In another analysis, Wall _et al_. showed a strong relationship between a student's choice of occupation, sorted according to type, and his Strong group score.

In yet another study, Kelso (1969) assessed 188 college males with the VPI and California Psychological Inventory (CPI), tested the ability of the VPI to discriminate across fields of study, and correlated VPI and CPI scale scores. The results indicated that students usually select courses consistent with their type and that types tend to have many of the personality traits attributed to them. In a similar study, Bohn (1966) related a student's psychological need scores from the Adjective Check List (Gough and Heilbrun, 1965) to his scales on the Strong (R = printer, I = chemist, A = artist, S = social science teacher, E = sales manager, and C = accountant). Although Bohn used only 75 college counseling clients, about one-third of his results were statistically significant. The expected association between types and needs, however, was only partially successful. In another study, Folsom (1969) assessed a sample of 1,003 college students with the College Student Questionnaires (Peterson, 1965) and then compared student types (defined by their choice of major field) on seven scales of the CSQ. The results lend support to the type formulations, except for the enterprising category.

Williams (1972) selected a random sample of 145 male graduate students from eighteen departments and sorted them according to type. Students were assessed by the VPI, the 16 PF, the Allport-Vernon-Lindzey Study of Values (AVL), and the Miller Occupational Values Indicator. Comparisons among types (using analysis of variance, multiple analysis of variance, multiple discriminant analysis, canonical correlations, and so on) indicated that a student's field of study (type) and his VPI, AVL, Miller Occupational, and 16 PF scores are usually consistent with the characteristics attributed to the types.

This complex and cleanly executed study is perhaps the best of its kind. The results are not only typically significant, but often of practical value. To illustrate, the application of discriminant analysis to the independent variables results in relatively efficient classifications of students. Using the VPI scales, 93 of 145 students are correctly classified according to fields of study. In the case of the AVL, 67 of 145 students are correctly classified, and the 16 PF scales correctly classify 83 of 145. The latter finding is especially important because it is strong evidence that field of study is partially dependent upon personality. These and other results replicate earlier findings and extend the characteristics associated with types to new variables.

Patterson, Marron, and Patterson (1971) tested some of the hypotheses about the social type. Occupational therapy students (N = 109), representing the social type, were administered the Edwards Personal Preference Schedule

(EPPS), the 16 PF, the Minnesota Multiphasic Personality Inventory (MMPI), the Tennessee Self-concept Scales, and the Firo-B. The results indicated that the occupational therapy students resembled the description for the social type.

Folsom (1971) assessed a sample of high school students (N = 366) with the VPI and CPI. The intercorrelations between these inventories provide only weak support for the hypothesized attributes of the types. And when students were categorized as types (according to their high-point VPI code) and compared on ranked CPI scales, the results were more negative than positive. Only 5 of 18 directional hypotheses were statistically significant, although 14 of 18 were in the predicted direction.

Several studies of employed adults suggest that the typology can be extended to the working population. Lacey (1971) used the VPI and a satisfaction scale to assess a sample of 210 men who were well established in their occupations. The VPI profiles obtained for eight subsamples of project engineers, research chemists, computer programmers, high school teachers, actuaries, executives, and college professors resembled profiles of college students interested in the same fields. His vocational needs and satisfaction analyses, however, were only partially successful and were sometimes ambiguous.

In a similar study, Hughes (1971) assessed 400 men aged 25 to 55 with the VPI, the SVIB, the 16 PF, a self-rating scale, the Sims Occupational Rating Scale, the Quick Word Intelligence Test, and a personal information blank. Using a man's occupation, Hughes categorized his subjects as types and performed multiple statistical analyses (principally chi-square) to test what characteristics were found for what types. The VPI scales placed 42 percent of the men in the correct occupational category; the SVIB predictions ranged from 14 to 35 percent using three different procedures; and the predictions obtained by using selected high and low scales of the 16 PF produced predictions only 23 percent correct. All these analyses were statistically significant, although they were generally not efficient. Self-ratings were not significantly related to types. Salomone (1968) assessed rehabilitation counselors with the VPI in an attempt to forecast their work behavior. Although the majority of counselors were social types according to the VPI, the other results were negative.

Several investigators have applied the theory to employed women. Werner (1969) administered the VPI and a survey to a sample of 348 women who were employed full time and ranged in age from 17 to 60. The VPI profiles for women employed in the six main categories were generally as expected. The main analyses (reported later) were usually equivocal or contrary to the hypothesis. Harvey (1971) administered the VPI, selected scales of the SVIB, the EPPS, the Allport-Vernon-Lindzey Study of Values, and the Differential Aptitude Tests to 61 adult women. Moderate relationships were obtained between types and their assumed characteristics, but some inconsistencies were observed.

Personality Patterns

The support for the hypotheses about personality patterns (profiles representing a person's resemblance to the types) and the hypotheses about the homogeneity and consistency of personality patterns is mixed. A brief review of the evidence about homogeneity and consistency follows.

Homogeneity (Differentiation). Only a few tests of this hypothesis have been made. Holland (1968b) categorized students as having profiles of high, middle, or low homogeneity (the difference between the highest and lowest VPI raw score), and then compared students for stability of vocational choice. For men, the results clearly support the hypothesis: Homogeneity is positively related to stability—that is, spiked profiles are stable and flat profiles are unstable (P < .05). The results for women were not significant. Another test of the homogeneity hypothesis in the same study consisted of examining the stability of vocational choice for students whose VPI profiles had (1) "no ties"—a single scale was higher than any other scale; (2) the two highest scales "tied"—both had equal scores; or (3) the three or more highest scales tied. The results of this analysis were also significant and according to expectation for men, but not for women. In the successful analysis, homogeneity increased the efficiency of prediction about 8 to 15 percent in a linear fashion. Tests of this hypothesis or other hypotheses about homogeneity by other investigators have nearly always been negative (W. E. Werner, 1969; Bates, Parker and McCoy, 1970; Kernen, 1971).

Consistency. Personality patterns that are consistent are assumed to forecast stability of vocational choice and achievement. There have been several tests of these hypotheses. Holland has shown that the consistency of a student's personality pattern (according to VPI profile) is positively related to the stability of a student's vocational choice or choice of major field over one- to four-year intervals (Holland, 1963; Holland, 1968b). These results were generally inefficient and held only for male samples. Other investigators (Hughes, 1971; Kernen, 1971) obtained either negative results or mixed and unimpressive results (J. E. Werner, 1969; W. E. Werner, 1969).

The most substantial and persuasive results for the usefulness of the concepts of homogeneity and consistency are given in Table 6. These simple analyses were performed to learn if the effects of consistency, homogeneity, and vocational role (ability to name a specific role in one's future occupation) are cumulative—that is, if their combined occurrence results in more efficient predictions. All possible combinations were tried. The results suggested that consistency, homogeneity, and vocational role preference cumulate to improve the prediction of vocational choice, but their relative contributions appear

TABLE 6
Prediction of Final Vocational Choice from Student's VPI Profile and Role Preference

VPI Profile				Fall		Samples (Males Only)			
						Spring		Fall-Int	
Consistency		Homogeneity	Preferred role	% Hits	f	% Hits	f	% Hits	f
C	+	Hi +	Explicit =	51.8	305	53.4	509	68.2	107
I	+	Hi +	Explicit =	52.2	115	53.0	185	54.4	49
C	+	Lo +	Explicit =	44.2	330	45.0	420	51.2	63
I	+	Lo +	Explicit =	45.0	160	37.3	233	47.5	56
C	+	Hi +	Ambiguous =	33.3	126	39.5	124	46.4	13
I	+	Hi +	Ambiguous =	26.2	42	32.1	56	30.0	10
C	+	Lo +	Ambiguous =	31.8	195	39.1	156	27.1	13
I	+	Lo +	Ambiguous =	25.6	86	28.9	90	19.4	6

Source: Holland, J.L. Explorations of a theory of vocational choice: VI. A longitudinal study using a sample of typical college students. *Journal of Applied Psychology*, 1968, 52, Table 27, 30. Copyright 1968 by the American Psychological Association, and reproduced by permission.

unequal. Explicit role preference contributes most to the prediction, followed by homogeneity and then by consistency. However, when these analyses were repeated by controlling for VPI high-point code of the largest subsample (investigative men), the results became clearer—so much so that they appeared contrived.

The results suggest a way to define vocational maturity or vocational adaptiveness in terms of the present theory. Vocationally mature people have consistent and homogeneous profiles and can enunciate a role within their future occupations. The results also reinforce some common notions about vocational counseling clients, particularly the notion that the row at the top of Table 6 describes the people vocational counselors rarely see, whereas the bottom row describes the typical client. In other words, most clients are those who produce confused interest profiles and who are unclear or uncertain about the vocational role they want to play.

More recently, Holland, Sorensen, Clark, Nafziger, and Blum (1973) have shown that the consistency of the occupational code of a man's first job predicts the category of his job five and ten years later. In contrast, men with inconsistent codes are not as predictable and become even less predictable over a ten-year interval. These findings appear important, for they are based upon a large subsample of a national representative sample of men in the United States.

Development

A few studies provide some fragmentary evidence about the development of a person's type and associated vocational interests. In an early study, Holland (1962) showed that a student's high-point VPI code was significantly related to the values and goals that fathers held for their sons and daughters. For example, a father who wanted his son to be "popular" was more apt to have a son with a peak on the enterprising scale; fathers who wanted their sons to be "curious" were more likely to have sons who peaked on the investigative or artistic scales. In another analysis using a different sample of bright students and their parents, additional small but significant relationships were obtained between a child's vocational interests and his mother's attitudes about child-rearing as assessed by the Parental Attitude Research Instrument (Schaeffer and Bell, 1958). The most obvious interpretation of the results (Holland, 1962, Table 18) is that conventional types (male and female) have mothers with the most authoritarian attitudes. Because fathers and sons had been administered VPIs (short and long forms), it was possible to test whether or not fathers and sons tended to have the same high-point codes or to be of the same type. Six by six chi-square tests were significant (P < .001), and the positive relationship is readily observable in the table based on 768 father-son pairs (Holland, 1962, Table 18). Finally, the effects of consistent attitudes between father and mother were analyzed for their relation to the child's vocational aspirations classified according to the typology. The analyses suggested that boys with realistic choices are more likely to have both parents with authoritarian attitudes, whereas boys with investigative choices are more likely to have both parents with democratic attitudes. These and other findings are significant, but the relationships are small and sometimes ambiguous. At best, they are only suggestive.

In an unpublished paper, Whitney (1970) successfully classified students as types using parental variables. Whitney used a sample of bright students (N = 295) to develop weights for classifying students according to centour scores. The weights derived from the first sample were then applied to a cross-validation sample (N = 575). The classification of students according to parental variables was only partially successful. The efficiency of the classification procedure was very low but significant. At the same time, small parent-child relationships are par for the course. The observation of stronger relationships between child and same-sex parent (as opposed to opposite-sex parent) also appears plausible.

More recently, Barclay (1972) found that parental occupation was associated with a broad range of student behaviors. Barclay assessed 1,386 elementary school children with the Barclay Classroom Climate Inventory (Barclay, 1970) and classified children as types and subtypes using paternal occupation. The simple analyses of variance for 29 variables for each student subtype strongly suggested that parental type (occupation) may encourage special outcomes in children, including their vocational interests, their sociometric choices of other children, and the teacher expectations they generate.

In a large-scale study of 127,125 students entering 248 four-year colleges, Werts and Watley (1970) compared paternal occupations with the probability of children's nonacademic scientific, artistic, oral, leadership, musical, and literary achievements in high school. The results clearly suggested that children excel at their fathers' occupational skills. For example, sons of scientists tended to win science contests, whereas sons of entrepreneurs had essentially zero probabilities of such success. These and other findings are impressive because they suggest the strong influence of family environment and heredity on a student's activities.

Searching Behavior

Earlier statements of the theory suggested that types "search" for congenial environments, but the hypotheses about types were not concerned with the actual searching activity. Now we do have a few studies that suggest how types search for environments.

Holland and Nichols (1964) found that people leave fields for which they lack interest and aptitude and seek fields for which they possess interest and aptitude. These are old conclusions, but this study documents them with a comprehensive assessment that provides both an objective and subjective picture of the process. In another study, Holland (1964) observed that students tended to be attracted to students like themselves. Subjects were asked to list the major fields of their three best friends. When a student's field was compared to the field of his best friend (listed first), the resulting 6 X 6 table was significant by chi-square test (P < .001 for men; P < .10 for women). In general, best friends shared the same major fields, or types were attracted to types. Identical analyses for each of the remaining friends produced similar 6 X 6 tables.

More recently, Hogan, Hall, and Blank (1971) extended the similarity-attraction hypothesis to activities and vocational interests. Using a standard experimental design for testing this hypothesis, they clearly demonstrated that students expect to like people who have interests similar to their own rather than people with divergent interests. This simple experimental study used a sample of 122 college students who were administered a brief interest and activities inventory to assess their resemblance to each of the types. The answer sheets were first sorted randomly into three groups, and then special answer sheets were constructed so that five weeks later each student received one of three kinds: (1) an answer sheet that was a copy of his own, (2) an answer sheet that agreed with half of his original responses, or (3) an answer sheet that was the opposite of his own. The students were asked to rate the person represented by the answer sheet on three items, using a 7-point scale. Three one-way analyses of variance were all significant (P < .001), and the mean ratings were in the expected order from high to low, without exception. In short, the subjects liked those who most resembled them in interests. The subjects also believed that people with interests similar to their own would be "enjoyable to work with," as well as "well adjusted."

Apostal (1970) has shown that students prefer those subcultures in their college that are consistent with their personality type. In a related study, Kipnis, Lane, and Berger (1967) found that "impulsive and restless" college students are attracted to business majors, whereas more controlled students are attracted to science and mathematics. These results imply that people search for environments that demand or support their more salient traits. For example, science and mathematics require day-to-day persistence and study; well-controlled people should therefore find science fields more congenial than business fields, which often demand impulsiveness. Other analyses indicate that bright science students with high-impulse scores get poorer grades and are less satisfied than bright science students with low impulse scores. A related study suggests that people are attracted to "familiar" jobs. Norman and Bessemer (1968) have shown that high school boys (N = 100) prefer familiar job titles to unfamiliar ones, regardless of the occupational prestige level. This "clinging to the familiar" persisted even when descriptive statements were used instead of job titles.

Finally, Andrews (1971) used a sample of 81 adults (aged 21 to 55) to demonstrate that there is a closer relationship between a man's future job and his current VPI code than between his current job and current VPI code

(P < .05). Andrews developed an elaborate procedure for measuring relatedness of personality pattern (VPI profile) and environment (job) by using the hexagonal model in Figure 3.

Occupational Perceptions

The assumption that people search for satisfying occupational environments implies that a person has a library of occupational stereotypes with a useful degree of reliability and validity. If stereotypical perceptions of occupations had no validity, people would have to devote enormous amounts of time to the acquisition of information so that they could cope successfully with the selection of their first and subsequent jobs.

Fortunately, a few investigators have made rapid progress with work that connects and supports these assumptions. In two major studies, O'Dowd and Beardslee (1960, 1967) showed that a sample of fifteen occupations are perceived in much the same way by a variety of large samples of faculty, college students, high school students, men, and women. They also demonstrated that although occupational stereotypes are complex, they can be organized in terms of a few factors which represent some of the common dimensions of occupations, especially status. They also showed that demographic differences make only small differences in the perception of occupations, and they found little change in stereotypes over four years of college.

Other studies support these findings and fill in more information about occupational stereotypes. Schutz and Blocher (1960), using a sample of 135 high school seniors, found that a student's vocational preference was significantly related to the "vocational sketch" (occupational stereotype) he had selected as self-descriptive one week earlier. They then suggested how the process of vocational choice might operate and why such stereotypes should have validity. In another study of 679 high school senior boys, Banducci (1968) found that a student's social status, academic potential, and vocational interests have a small rather than a large influence on the accuracy of his occupational stereotypes. At the same time, Banducci extended the work of O'Dowd and Beardslee (1967) and Grunes (1957) by suggesting how several personal characteristics operate in expected ways. For example, bright students had more accurate stereotypes of higher-level jobs, and poor students had more accurate stereotypes of lower-level jobs. In addition, students tended to have more accurate perceptions of occupations that corresponded to the dominant scale in their vocational interest profile (VPI). In short, Banducci's work illustrates how selective perception functions in a person's occupational search according to type and demographic characteristics.

More recently, Marks and Webb (1969) demonstrated that students entering the fields of industrial management or electrical engineering possess "a fairly accurate image of the typical incumbent of the intended occupation."

Their elaborate study was of two occupational titles by three levels of experience—freshmen, seniors, and professionals before, during, and after training. The earlier study by Banducci (1968) contained a Range of Experience Scale that was unrelated to the accuracy of a student's occupational stereotypes when the effects of social status and academic potential were held constant.

In other studies, Holland (1963-64) has shown that students perceive occupational titles representing the types in stereotypical ways and that students rate the typical person in their future occupation in accordance with the formulations for the types (Holland, 1964). In an elegant study, Hollander and Parker (1969) had 54 high school students describe six occupations (one per type) using the Adjective Check List (Gough and Heilbrun, 1965). A single-factor analysis of variance with repeated measures was used to determine the degree of consistency in the student descriptions. Every ACL need scale (15) was significant (F test) across the six occupations, and student stereotypes were generally consistent with the formulations for the types.

Other investigators (Crutchfield, Woodworth, and Albrecht, 1958; Osipow, 1969) have shown that vocational interests (SVIB and VPI scales) are correlated with objective perceptual tests, associative flexibility, word-sorting, extreme response sets, and closure flexibility. The results of these investigations are provocative, but so far they have failed to cumulate findings in a consistent and persuasive manner.

Taken together, these studies of occupational images strongly suggest that stereotypes are stable over time, have validity, and to a lesser degree are selectively perceived according to social status, intelligence, and degree of involvement in the occupation in question. Equally important, occupations seen as representing particular types are seen in ways that appear consistent with characteristics attributed to the types.

Direction of Vocational Choice

Predictions of what kind of occupation a person will select when his type is assessed by VPI scales, SVIB scales, or personal sketches have always been statistically significant but only moderately efficient. Predictions from VPI scales have ranged from 25 to 51 percent correct identification, depending upon the type and occupational category in question and the time interval for the prediction—one to two years (Holland, 1962, 1968b). Predictions from SVIB scales selected to assess the types have usually been less efficient—26 to 28 percent for a four-year interval. Concurrent relationships (SVIB vs. vocational choice) are higher—21 to 33 percent (Holland, 1963; Hughes, 1971).

The six VPI scales used to represent the types are useful for discriminating across educational and vocational groups or occupations. Studies by Abe and Holland (1965a, 1965b), Scott and Sedlacek (1968), Holland (1966a, 1968b), Brue (1969), Wall (1969, 1971), Williams (1972), and others using different procedures provide ample demonstration of the discriminative power of these scales.

In contrast, the prediction of vocational choice from qualitative data—choice of field of study, employment status, expressed choice of occupation—categorized according to type has usually been more efficient than predictions from the VPI. For a whole sample, the efficiency of the VPI rarely exceeds 45 percent—a gain of about 28 to 29 percent over the usual expected efficiency. Over eight to twelve months, Holland (1968b) found that a student's initial choice of occupation, categorized according to type, was about twice as efficient or about 63 to 86 percent for the different types. Elton and Rose (1970) studied the vocational migrations of university students over a four-year interval and obtained similar results. For a sample of 530, the percentage of hits per type or category ranges from 49 to 87 percent for predictions made from the category of a student's freshman choice. For the same sample, the percentage of hits per type or category ranges from only 9 to 41 percent for the ACT Admission Tests and the Omnibus Personality Inventory organized by a step-wise multiple discriminant analysis. Kelso (1969) and others have obtained similar results in comparisons of the predictive efficiency of the VPI versus expressed vocational choice.

Level of Vocational Choice

The first formulation for the level of occupational choice or achievement (Holland, 1959) was that occupational level equals intelligence plus self-evaluation. This formulation has been used by several investigators, and in every instance it has led to positive and often efficient results. Stockin (1964), Hughes (1971), Schutz and Blocher (1961), Holland (1962), and Fortner (1970) have substituted different measures in the formula and employed different statistical analyses.

To simplify the theory, the formula for the level of occupational choice was reformulated in terms of personality patterns (Holland, 1966b). In that formulation, the more a person resembles enterprising and social types, the more likely he is to have higher aspirations, to achieve more, and to be occupationally more mobile. In the current statement the formulation is more explicit (see page 25): The closer a person's resemblance to the personality pattern ESAICR, the greater his expected vocational aspiration and eventual achievement.

The first test of the current formulation produced substantial results. The initial occupational code for a national, representative sample of men was used to predict their occupational status five and ten years later (Holland, Sorensen, Clark, Nafziger, and Blum, 1973). Occupational status was defined as job prestige. The rank-order correlation between the expected and observed level of occupational prestige was .52 and .61 for five- and ten-year intervals.

Typological Definitions

The use of the VPI to define types and personality patterns in theoretical studies and for other research purposes has extended the meaning of the VPI scales to many unanticipated variables and personal characteristics. These varied uses of the VPI have served to clarify the meanings of the types because more multimethod and multitrait correlational matrixes have become available. Consequently, the use of the VPI for typing persons is supported by an extensive base of divergent and convergent validity, as the following paragraphs show.

Several investigators have correlated the VPI and the SVIB scales using simple or canonical correlations or both. For example, Haase (1971) correlated 6 VPI scales and 47 scales of the SVIB and found that 100 percent of the trace was extracted by six canonical roots. The six canonical correlations for a sample of 176 male college students ranged from .66 to .86. Haase concludes that the VPI and SVIB measure similar dimensions. Other researchers (Lee, 1970; Cockriel, 1972) have correlated the VPI and Strong, scale by scale, and obtained positive evidence that these inventories cover similar ground and do so almost precisely according to expectation. And Rezler (1967) found that the VPI and the Kuder intercorrelate according to the predictions in Table 1.

Campbell (1971) and Campbell and Holland (1972) developed an alternate male form of the VPI by selecting Strong items in accordance with the definitions of the types. These six a priori scales of equal length were then used to rescore the occupational samples in the Strong archives. The classification of 76 occupations according to the mean scores of employed adults on this alternate form of the VPI and according to the actual mean VPI scores of aspirants to the same occupations (Holland, Whitney, Cole, and Richards, 1969) resulted in 84 percent agreement among the six main categories. This outcome is clear evidence that aspirants to occupations closely resemble incumbents, that the definitions of the types are not dependent upon the idiosyncrasies of the VPI, and that the Strong data strengthen the formulations for the types and their associated classification.

Hansen and Johansson (1972) developed an alternate form of the VPI for scoring the women's Strong blank. Their scale-construction method parallels the method used by Campbell and Holland (1972). The application of the six typological scales to 92 criterion samples of employed women (median sample size, 200) arranges occupations "in a common sense and meaningful sequence over a range of about two standard deviations."

Apostal and Harper (1972) have provided an indirect test of the typological definitions. These investigators categorized both Strong Basic Interest Scales and major fields of study according to type. Their simple analyses of variance for 203 college students indicated that five of the six Basic Interest Scales discriminated across student types ($P < .001$). Other investigators (Blakeney, Matteson, and Holland, 1972) have provided more direct evidence that the alternate VPI (Campbell, 1971) and the original VPI (Holland, 1965) are moderately correlated with one another and in clear patterns of divergent and convergent validity.

Baird (1970) has shown that the VPI scores are moderately related to a person's life goals, self-ratings of ability and personality traits, and potential for achievement. Baird used a national sample of 11,249 men and 9,120 women attending thirty-seven liberal arts colleges, state universities, teachers colleges, and two-year colleges. Students were assessed with the VPI, 31 self-ratings of common traits, 35 self-ratings of life goals, 10 competence scales, and other measures of potential and background. Canonical correlations between the VPI scores and the major kinds of student variables ranged from .20 to .70. The correlations between the VPI and the nonacademic achievement scales were generally the highest. Because his sample was large and diverse, Baird provides the most substantial evidence that assessment of types by the VPI incorporates comprehensive information about a person. Salomone and Muthard (1972) have shown that a few scales of the VPI and the Minnesota Importance Questionnaire (vocational needs) are related. Their results (a single significant canonical correlation of .52) suggest that the VPI and the MIQ have only one overlapping dimension. And Dayton and Uhl (1966) found that a high school student's VPI scales were "as efficient a predictor of classroom achievement as the teacher's rating of the student's classroom behavior" (Multiple Rs ranged from .50 to .77).

Several additional studies provide more information about the power of the VPI scales to discriminate among well-defined groups. Osipow and Ashby (1968), using a sample of 831 male and 129 female college freshmen, showed that VPI high-point codes usually identify a student's educational preference. Brue (1969) showed that the VPI scales differentiate community college transfer and occupational groups with moderate efficiency. In a longitudinal study of engineering students and their migrations through a large university, Krulee, O'Keefe, and Goldberg (1966) demonstrated that an abbreviated form of the VPI (66 items, or only 6 items per scale) was moderately efficient in differentiating student groups and predicting migration.

Johansson (1971) rescored the SVIBs for the alternate form of the VPI (Campbell, 1971) for large samples of students at three institutions and for successive samples of entering freshmen at each institution over an eight-year period. The graphs formed from these data for each type appear consistent with some trends in admissions, and the differences between institutions appear plausible. The differences between student samples and the men-in-general sample, which Johansson provides, are likewise usually instructive.

Some indirect tests of the definition of types have been made by several researchers. Lee (1970) classified 432 male college freshmen according to the high-point code of their VPI and then treated these six subsamples as separate populations. For each sample, Lee used canonical correlations and a multiple linear regression equivalent of analysis of covariance to predict grades and achievement scores from the SVIB and the VPI scores. The outcomes suggested that appropriate Strong or VPI scales (physicist for investigative, accountant for conventional, and so on) only occasionally predict according to theoretical expectations. The results of this elaborate study are, however, especially difficult to interpret. At best, they appear to give some weak support to the definition of types in VPI terms, for Lee reports more negative than positive results.

In a similar study using the same sample, Lee and Hedahl (1972) obtained significant and substantial results. When students were categorized according to their VPI high-point code and compared on the Basic Interest (BI) scales of the SVIB, the BI scales discriminated among the types with moderate efficiency: "Twenty-one of the 22 F tests and 19 of the Scheffe multiple comparisons among the means were significant." In particular, BI scales usually peaked according to the formulations for the types; for instance, enterprising students had the highest mean on public speaking.

Another indirect test of the definitions of types was performed by Kristjanson (1969). A sample of 255 college counseling clients were categorized as types by using Strong profiles. Then simple analyses of variance across the types for 15 Edwards Personal Preference Schedule scales revealed that 7 of the 15 EPPS needs were statistically significant. In addition, 47 of 54 directional hypotheses were in the predicted direction, and 25 of the 47 were significant. These and other analyses provide powerful indirect evidence that the definition of types via categories has the expected validity. A similar attempt to test the definitions of types by categorizing students in terms of the Strong Basic scales and comparing the resulting six types with the EPPS was largely negative (Bailey, 1971). These results can be attributed to a small sample with a narrow range of talent, interests, and SES (135 National Merit semifinalists attending the University of Kansas).

Using correlational matrixes obtained from the use of the Self-directed Search (Holland, 1971b), Edwards and Whitney (1972) performed several factor analyses—separate analyses for each of the four domains (activities, competencies, occupations, and self-ratings) and for the total 30 X 30 matrices. They usually found that the same main factors existed within each domain and that the patterns of factor loadings were similar from one domain to the next. Taken together, the multiple factor analyses imply that the personality types can be assessed in one or more of four domains, and the first definitions of the types based on the VPI scales probably can be interchanged with definitions based on other domains with only minor errors. The clear patterns of convergent and discriminant validity in the original correlational matrixes for men and women reinforce the same conclusion (see Edwards and Whitney, 1972, Table 1, p. 4). In a related study, Richards (in Holland, 1968a) performed diagonal factor analyses to determine the degree to which each VPI scale is independent of what all the scales have in common. The results of separate analyses for large samples (3,771 men and 3,492 women) clearly demonstrated that each scale does measure something different. There are at least six kinds of people; there may be more, but there are not fewer.

ENVIRONMENTAL MODELS

The hypotheses about the environmental models have attracted only a few investigators, and their efforts have been devoted mostly to educational environments. The evidence about environments (direct and indirect) has been categorized as educational or occupational.

Educational Environments

In an extensive series of reports, Astin and his colleagues have tested the general hypothesis that the environment of an undergraduate institution can be known by the distribution of student types at that institution. Using the environmental assessment technique (EAT) described on page 33, Astin and Holland (1961) learned that the student description of a college obtained from the College Characteristics Index could be predicted from the percentages of the six student types attending the college. Such descriptions were reliable accounts over one to six years; reliability coefficients ranged from .54 to .97, with a median of .93.

In another test of the environmental assessment technique, Astin (1963) polled students in seventy-six colleges (15 to 216 students per college) for their perceptions of the college environment and its effects: "Mean responses to 14 of the 18 college environment items were significantly related to EAT variables in the predicted direction," and "15 of the 21 perceived effects of college were significantly related to at least one EAT variable." For example, "all items pertaining to the importance of social groups and interpersonal skills . . . tended to be negatively related to" the investigative dimension of the EAT. The relationships between student perceptions and the remaining five EAT variables were less successful.

In other studies, Astin has been only peripherally concerned with validating the Environmental Assessment Technique, but he has accumulated substantial evidence that the EAT variables, principally in his weighted version, assess large portions of influential variance in the environment and correlate with many of its objective features. Astin (1964) has found that the characteristics of entering freshmen can be predicted with moderate efficiency from the EAT variables for a college and that the EAT variables are correlated with freshmen variables in expected ways. In another study, Astin (1965a) reports significant relationships between the popularity and selectivity of an institution and its EAT variables.

In a more analytical article, Astin (1965b) assessed classroom environments to learn whether or not consistent differences would be found among the
different fields of study. Student ratings of introductory courses in nineteen
fields were obtained from 4,109 students at 246 institutions. Differences among
the nineteen fields on all 35 ratings were statistically significant, and the
differences among fields were often large. These and other results strengthen the
main assumptions underlying the EAT: (1) The environments in different fields
are different. (2) The characteristics of instructors representing a field may
resemble our theoretical expectations. In the present study, "instructors in
accounting ranked above instructors in all other fields in frequency of taking
attendance, in having their classes meet at a regularly scheduled time and place,
in following the textbook closely in their lectures, and in being judged as
'speaking in a monotone.' " (3) The college environment is probably affected by
the distribution of students and faculty in different fields of study.

In his book *The College Environment* (1968), Astin also indicates that the
EAT variables have substantial and plausible relationships to numerous
subjective and objective aspects of college environments. His guide to colleges,
Who Goes Where to College? (1965d), also summarizes many relationships
between the EAT variables and a wide range of students and institutional
characteristics (see Astin, 1965d, Appendix E, p. 115).

In another group of reports, Richards and others have used the EAT
variables (Astin and Holland, 1961) to assess two-year colleges, four-year
colleges, and graduate school environments. In addition to classifying students
according to field, Richards has extended the EAT concepts by using the
number of faculty and the number of curriculums, classified according to field,
as methods for assessing environments.

In their first study, Richards, Seligman, and Jones (1970) obtained EAT
profiles for undergraduate and graduate environments. For each environment,
individual EAT profiles were obtained for curriculum (number of course
offerings in each of six areas), faculty (number of faculty in each area), and
students (number of students graduating in each area). To obtain comparable
scores for curriculum, faculty, and students, the authors converted scores for
each kind of assessment to normalized standard scores. The results revealed that
these three methods for assessing a college environment produce similar findings.
The profiles obtained from the curriculum and faculty are also relatively stable
for a twenty-year interval. The correlations between the faculty EAT scores for a
college and the scores obtained from Astin's institutional factors, from his
weighted EAT variables for students, and from the scores of Pace's College and
University Environment Scales (CUES) support the construct validity of the
faculty EAT measures: "More than half of the correlations are significant, and
each of the other environmental measures is significantly correlated with several
faculty, curriculum, and degrees profile scores." Table 7, taken from Richards,

TABLE 7
Correlations between Faculty Profile Scores and Environmental Measures Developed by Others

Environmental Measures	Faculty Profile Scores							
	Elevation	Scatter	Realistic	Intellectual	Social	Conventional	Enterprising	Artistic
College and University Environment Scales[a]								
Practicality	26**	-25**	04	-43**	25**	06	-26**	12
Community	-65**	-28**	-38**	-18	12	33**	-11	38**
Awareness	16	-09	-22**	-11	17	-11	19*	19*
Propriety	-42**	-12	-32**	-29**	29**	36**	-27**	25**
Scholarship	-12	05	13	39**	-27**	-13	09	-15
Astin (1956)[b]								
Intellectualism	00	19*	35**	59**	-52**	-28**	21*	-31**
Estheticism	-03	20*	01	06	-08	-09	05	10
Status	-13	00	-24**	13	-13	-25**	54**	24**
Pragmatism	44**	09	68**	40**	-40**	-36**	-01	-55**
Masculinity	08	04	23**	40**	-42**	-20*	35**	-29**
Selectivity	09	31**	25**	44**	-39**	-23**	22**	-23**
Size	94**	23**	33**	-06	02	-33**	03	-18*
Realistic orientation	46**	05	72**	35**	-34**	-33**	-16*	-53**
Intellectual orientation	-24**	02	31**	57**	-48**	-18*	09	-28**
Social orientation	-08	-09	-48**	-59**	65**	31**	-27**	38**
Conventional orientation	31**	-17*	-08	-17*	05	-18*	36**	08
Enterprising orientation	-09	-09	-28**	-01	-04	-21*	53**	26**
Artistic orientation	-15	06	-57**	-39**	32**	20*	12	55**
Astin (1962)[c]								
Affluence	-10	17	24*	55**	-36**	-32**	24*	-22*
Size	88**	00	34**	-11	15	-26**	-16	-29**
Masculinity	27*	-24*	41**	30**	-31**	-27*	12	-35**
Homogeneity	-50**	28*	-07	22*	-30**	38**	-05	-06
Realistic	61**	13	66**	14	-14	-33**	-37**	-41**

[a]N = 106. *P < .05.
[b]N = 139. **P < .01.
[c]N = 78.

Source: Richards, J.M., Jr., Seligman, R., and Jones, P.W. Faculty and curriculum as measures of college environment. *Journal of Educational Psychology*, 1970, 61, 324-332. Copyright 1970 by the American Psychological Association, and reproduced by permission.

Seligman, and Jones (1970), summarizes these relationships. Similar analyses of 87 graduate school catalogs revealed that EAT profiles for graduate degrees, faculty, and curriculums were positively intercorrelated, and that the CUES scales were usually related to graduate school EAT measures in consistent ways (more detail is given in Richards and Seligman, 1969).

These studies are valuable not only because they extend the EAT concepts to new populations or sources of data, but also because the new techniques do not confuse student characteristics with environmental measures. Since the original EAT measures used students only, interaction studies employing the EAT variables based on student types may have been studies of only student characteristics, rather than studies of student and environmental variables. In addition, these new scoring procedures "make it possible to study new problems such as the history of college environments or international differences in college environments." In a related study, Richards, Bulkeley, and Richards (1971) characterized the faculty and curriculums of 94 two-year colleges. Again, they obtained positive results. EAT scores based on faculty, curriculum, and student degrees for the six areas corresponding to the types were positively intercorrelated; correlations ranged from .27 to .82, with a median r of .52. In addition, the three techniques for assessing the EAT variables correlated with environmental factor variables obtained in another study of two-year colleges (Richards, Rand, and Rand, 1966).

Richards (1971) has also characterized 124 Japanese colleges and universities by performing a factor analysis of their institutional characteristics and by classifying their faculty according to type. When the faculty scores representing the EAT variables are correlated with the factor analytic variables of institutional characteristics, the results are similar to those obtained in American institutions (Richards, Bulkeley, and Richards, 1971; Richards, Seligman, and Jones, 1970). Over half the correlations are statistically significant, and each environmental measure is correlated with several profile scores. Equally important, the correlations are, with few exceptions, consistent with the formulations for the environmental models.

Barclay (1967) developed a method for assessing the "teacher-press" or the teacher environment for eleven different high school curriculums. Teachers nominated students who most and least conformed to their notions of ideal students. High- and low-rated students were then compared on 80 intellective, personality, motivational, and vocational variables. Using Holland's classification, Barclay found that "the direction of environmental press in each curriculum" was often predictable from Holland's formulations, but that there were many contradictions. For example, the students rated "high" by business education teachers were ESCs and the students rated "low" were SERs (as assessed by the VPI). Barclay's results also show that similar secondary and college curriculums have similar VPI profiles or codes.

Occupational Environments

The construct validity of the EAT measures has been strengthened by showing that a great range of objective, environmental, and personal characteristics associated with individual occupations have strong and consistent relationships with groups of occupations when they are organized according to the model environments. The factor analytic investigations of the Dictionary of Occupational Titles, standard and special job analyses (McCormick, Jeanneret, and Mecham, 1969; Jeanneret and McCormick, in press) made it possible to learn how the EAT variables are related to both personal and environmental measures developed to characterize the full range of occupational environments.

This task was accomplished by categorizing each of 832 occupations as one of six kinds. Then simple analyses of variance tests were performed for each of 32 occupational factors (McCormick and Jeanneret, in press). The results provide clear evidence that the Holland environmental categories, developed almost entirely from psychological data, also encompass more objective, situational data about jobs (see Table 8, page 76).

Other environmental data also imply that the EAT has validity (Borgen, Weiss, Tinsley, Dawis, and Lofquist, 1968). These investigators obtained occupational reinforcer patterns (ORPs) for 81 occupations. The ORPs, consisting of 21 environmental influences and opportunities, are based on the ratings of 2,976 supervisors of jobs in several hundred companies. The authors also arranged the 81 occupations in nine clusters or groups of similar jobs that resemble the six EAT variables. If the ORPs for the 81 occupations are reorganized according to the Holland classification, the reinforcer patterns for the resulting six groups appear congruent with the formulations in Chapter 3.

INTERACTIONS

The theory has been applied to the person-environment interactions of high school, college, and graduate students, as well as to those of several adult groups. The results of these studies are difficult to interpret because they rely on the validity of the formulations for both types and environmental models as well as their operational definitions. In addition, large Ns of people or institutions are often required to satisfy most experimental designs. Despite these obstacles, some coherent findings have been obtained.

High School Students

Werner (1969) selected a sample of 527 boys and girls from a population of 1,445 students in seven occupational training centers. Students from six occupational areas were selected to represent each type: auto mechanics for realistic, technical electronics for investigative, practical nursing for social, data processing for conventional, distributive education for enterprising, and commercial art for artistic. An additional 67 students who had left these programs were available for analyses of attrition.

Students were assessed with the VPI, the Kuder, and questionnaires about occupational concerns and achievement. In this study, the special occupational training was treated as the environment. For example, auto mechanics training equaled a realistic environment. A boy who peaked on the realistic scale of the VPI and who was training as an auto mechanic was in a congruent environment. Using this definition of congruence and the standard definitions of consistency and homogeneity (differentiation) for a student's VPI profile, Werner obtained the following results:

1. Students in congruent environments had higher achievement scores than students in incongruent environments.
2. Congruence was related to satisfaction for boys but not for girls.
3. Congruence was related to remaining in a program.
4. Consistency and homogeneity of a student's VPI profile yielded inconsistent and negative results.
5. Consistency, congruence, and homogeneity were found to be additive for achievement but not for satisfaction.

In many ways, Werner's recent study reiterates many trends and problems found in earlier studies—positive support for the general hypothesis about congruence of type and environment, but mixed results for most other hypotheses.

College Students

Several investigators have studied the effect of congruence upon achievement, satisfaction with college, stability of vocational choice, personal adjustment, and other outcomes. Among these studies, one of the most dramatic and convincing is a simple experiment by Williams (1967).

Williams examined a familar problem in the present theoretical context—conflict between freshmen male roommates as a study of congruent or incongruent interactions. Because all entering freshmen were administered the VPI, Williams was able to locate 39 roommate pairs who were reported "in conflict" (according to housing staff) or who separated because of "conflict." Another 39 roommate pairs with no evidence of conflict were selected randomly from a population of 131 nonconflict pairs. All pairs in this study had been assigned to common double rooms. When the data is arranged in a 2 X 2 table, congruence of student codes is positively associated with lack of conflict ($P < .05$). And among the student pairs "in conflict," the most common pattern of VPI codes is investigative-enterprising (8 of 39).

This simple study is difficult to fault since all available data were used, environments were standard (common double rooms), the criterion of conflict was overt enough to be assessed by outsiders, the assignment of roommates was random, and so on. A less analytical experiment by Brown (1966) also suggests that different kinds of peers provide different kinds of reinforcement. In the Brown experiment, the proportions of peers with science or nonscience goals on a student's dorm floor clearly influenced a student's tendency to maintain or change goals. In this study, students in the minority fields (only 25 percent were in science) tended to move to majority fields (75 percent were in nonscience) when both groups lived on the same floor of a dormitory. The reverse situation also held. When nonscience students (25 percent) lived with science students (75 percent), nonscience students tended to switch to science fields. In theoretical terms, science majors equaled realistic and investigative types, and nonscience students equaled the remaining types. The results suggest how types in the majority manipulate types in the minority.

Posthuma and Navran (1970) tested the hypothesis that students whose interests were congruent with the faculty would get better grades than students with incongruent interests. The investigators administered the VPI to all available first year students (N = 110) and 88 percent of the faculty (N = 44) at a military college. A discriminant analysis indicated that the VPI could be used to discriminate student groups at four grade levels. Comparisons of faculty with students at each grade level were also significant (Mahalanobis D^2), but the trends were not consistent with congruence. A comparison of the modal VPI profiles for faculty versus the modal profiles of students at four levels of academic achievement were generally as predicted, but not significant. Profiles for faculty and "top students" correlated (rank-order) .69; profiles for faculty and "failure students" correlated −.26.

Holland (1968b) used a sample of 2,347 college students at twenty-seven colleges and universities to test some hypotheses about stability of vocational choice and satisfaction with college. A student's initial choice of vocation was used to characterize him as a type, and the EAT was used to define the environment. Several analyses provided weak support for the congruence hypothesis—students tended to maintain their vocational choices when their college was dominated by students whose choices belonged to the same general class. Weak support was also obtained for the hypothesis that homogeneous environments are conducive to vocational stability. And conflicting findings were received for the hypothesis that a student's satisfaction with his college will be greater if his type is congruent with his college environment: the results were negative for men and positive for women. Finally, the average satisfaction score at a college was negatively correlated with the homogeneity (differentiation) of the college environment: Students "are more likely to be satisfied in colleges characterized by their flat profiles—about equal percentages of personality types."

Elton (1971) provided indirect evidence about the interaction of types and environments. Using small college student samples, Elton showed that students who left engineering underwent personality changes that made them different from students who remained in the engineering environment. In contrast to students remaining in engineering, "students transferring to arts and sciences become more realistic, non-judgmental, intellectually liberal, and skeptical of orthodox religious beliefs." Comparisons of university students with students in two-year colleges implied similar expected environmental effects. For example, two-year college students showed the smallest change on the variable of scholarly orientation.

Privateer (1971) examined the effect of a college environment upon entering freshmen. Upon entry, Privateer assessed all freshmen (N = 600) with the VPI. Then an "established population" of administrative staff, randomly selected faculty, juniors, and seniors were administered the VPI and CUES. After an eight-month exposure to campus life, the freshmen were again administered the VPI along with a questionnaire and the CUES for the first time. A student's congruence with his environment (his VPI versus EAT for the college) was not significantly different from fall to spring. Student profiles did not become more consistent, but the homogeneity (differentiation) of student profiles did increase. These and other results were generally negative.

Although Astin (1965c) and Astin and Panos (1969) have been primarily concerned with estimating the effects of educational environments, their work also lends support to the present hypothesis about person-environment interactions, because they use the Holland typology in some analyses to characterize students and college environments. In an early study of college influence, Astin (1965c) used 17 student (precollege) variables to control for student input, and found "some support for the hypothesis that the student's career choice comes to conform more and more to the . . . modal career choice in his college environment." In their major substantive study involving 36,000 students at 246 institutions, Astin and Panos (1969) came to the same conclusion. Table 57, page 119, of their study gives a summary of the environmental characteristics that affect vocational choice. It shows that the EAT variables influence vocational choice, but that a host of other environmental variables are also potent influences and often more important.

Walsh and Lacey (1969, 1970), in separate studies of men (N = 151) and women (N = 157), examined how students change over four years of college by asking students to estimate how they have changed on rating scales of adjectives, traits, and abilities. The results suggest that students of a given type (defined by their field of study) become more like that type. Although their results hold only for three types for men and four types for women, the findings are consistent with the hypothesis that an environment dominated by a particular type reinforces the same type. In a similar study, Walsh, Vaudrin, and Hummel (1972) found that college seniors report more change consistent with their personality type than freshmen do. Another study (Walsh and Barrow, 1971) designed to test the personality differences between students who make congruent or incongruent choices of major field produced negative results. And Walsh and Russell (1969) found that students who had made a congruent choice of college major (student's high-point VPI code and choice of field belong to same category in Holland's classification) reported fewer personal adjustment problems than students who had made incongruent choices. This finding is consistent with the hypothesis that congruence encourages personal stability.

A recent study by Walsh and Lewis (1972) reinforces some earlier findings and has a strong design. The investigators categorized a student's choice of field in college as congruent, incongruent, or undecided. Congruent students (37 males and 37 females) peaked on VPI scales that were congruent with their choice of field—for instance, high-point VPI code is "investigative" and choice of field is "physics." Incongruent students (37 males and 37 females) peaked on VPI scales that were incongruent with their choice—for example, "conventional" and "art." And undecided students had failed to make a choice. These three groups were administered the Omnibus Personality Inventory (Heist and Yonge, 1968) and then compared scale by scale using analysis of variance.

The statistically significant results imply that congruent males, as opposed to incongruent or undecided males, report "few attitudes associated with social alienation or emotional disturbance" (personal integration scale), "few feelings or symptoms of anxiety" (anxiety level scale), and many responses associated with making a good impression on the inventory (response-bias scale). These results appear consistent with the hypothesized effects of person-environment congruence—maintenance of personal stability and satisfaction. These findings also suggest that stability of vocational choice occurs through integration with others and subsequent reinforcement. The results for women were sometimes statistically significant but often ambiguous. However, sex differences on single scales are usually in accord with past evidence and stereotypes about men and women.

Morrow (1971) used samples of college students (N = 323) majoring in mathematics or sociology to test the hypothesis that satisfaction with one's field depends upon the congruence of type and field. Morrow's results were mixed: Satisfaction with major was significantly related to personality type for mathematics students but not for sociology students.

Frantz and Walsh (1972) applied the theory to graduate student-institution interactions. These investigators tested the usefulness of different definitions of congruence, consistency, and homogeneity (differentiation), and the effects of these variables on satisfaction and achievement. Most findings were negative, ambiguous, or weak. The new definitions of consistency, homogeneity and congruence appear more useful than the old, but the evidence is not strong. The most important and clearest finding is that students who are congruent, consistent, and homogeneous (differentiated) are more satisfied and achieve more than students who do not possess all these characteristics (see Frantz and Walsh, 1972, Table 4).

An attempt to use the typology (VPI profiles) to forecast the outcomes of educational-vocational counseling, counselor-client interactions, and academic performance in college produced only negative findings (Ingram, 1969). The sample of 304 "marginally-achieving" students may have represented too small a range of types and ability for the theory. Nevertheless, this study wins the award for the study with the most comprehensive and explicit set of negative findings. A well-designed study by Whitney and Whittlesey (1972) in which counseling outcomes were predicted for different student types was also generally negative: "Exceptions were in the number of counseling interviews (where Investigative clients had the most sessions) and the degree of counselor's personal liking for client (counselors liked clients with moderately consistent profiles better than those with inconsistent profiles)."

Employed Adults

Bates, Parker, and McCoy (1970) tested several hypotheses about the congruence of person-environment interactions and obtained only negative results. Why the hypotheses about congruence, consistency, and homogeneity failed to hold for their sample of 259 vocational rehabilitation cases is unclear, although the subjects represent only 12 percent of the population sampled.

A study of clergymen by Osipow (1970) showed that the actual work roles of clergymen were unrelated to their type, although the majority of clergymen were characterized as social types by the VPI. The hypotheses about homogeneity produced statistically significant but somewhat ambiguous findings. Because Osipow did not actually assess both person and environment by independent means, this study is only an indirect analysis of person-environment interactions.

CLASSIFICATION

The theory's classification system is used to categorize people, occupations, or environments as types or subtypes. The classification includes six main categories corresponding to the types, and each main category contains five to sixteen subcategories, such as realistic-investigative-artistic, realistic-investigative-social, and so on. Because the classification is an integral part of the theory, the act of classification makes it possible to use the theory to interpret or predict the behavior and activities of persons and the influence of occupations or environments assigned to a particular category. For example, a person categorized as an RIE should exhibit the characteristics of the realistic type most, the investigative type next, and so on. Occupations categorized as RIE should encourage realistic activities, competencies, perceptions, and so on.

The following sections summarize the development of the classification and some tests of its usefulness or validity. Appendix B contains the current revision of the classification.

Development

This section gives the history of the classification and its revisions from 1959 to 1972. In general, the goals of the following studies were usually to create a classification with ideal characteristics (comprehensiveness, independence of categories, classification by a single principle). The different stages in the development of the classification have been categorized as preliminary classifications, an intermediate classification, and the current classification.

Preliminary classifications. In 1959, an a priori classification of six categories was proposed (Holland, 1959):

1. Realistic (technical, skilled, and laboring occupations)
2. Intellectual (scientific occupations)
3. Social (educational and social welfare occupations)
4. Conventional (office and clerical occupations)
5. Enterprising (sales and managerial occupations)
6. Artistic (artistic, literary, and musical occupations)

From 1959 to 1965 this classification was used in several theoretical studies, but it was neither directly tested for its value as a classification system nor explicitly defined for clear and easy use.

Later, Holland (1966a, 1966b) defined the major categories of the classification—realistic, intellectual, social, conventional, enterprising, and artistic—in terms of the six Vocational Preference Inventory (VPI) scales having the same names. The VPI is a brief inventory of a person's interests consisting of 160 occupational titles (Holland, 1965). People take the inventory by indicating the occupations they "like" or "dislike." Each occupational title is assigned to a scale or category; for example, "bank teller" is assigned to the conventional category. Thus the VPI scales consist of six groups of occupations, one group for each scale or occupational class.

The assumption that each occupational title in the VPI can be classified into one of the six categories in the classification made it possible to reconstruct the classification scheme in an explicit manner. The VPI was administered to students planning to enter different professions. The mean number of occupations rated "like" was calculated for each scale (realistic, intellectual, and so on) for all students planning to enter a given occupation. VPI profiles were then formed for each occupation by placing the highest scale mean first, the next highest mean second, and so on. The results defined an occupation's place in the classification. For example, the majority of students planning to be civil engineers obtained a profile of RIE; "civil engineer" was thus placed in the major category realistic, and in the subcategory realistic-intellectual-enterprising. This procedure was applied to the VPI data for 12,432 college freshmen in thirty-one institutions (Abe and Holland, 1965a), and produced separate occupational classifications for men and women.

As a next step, Holland, Whitney, Cole, and Richards (1969) added VPI data for a sample of two-year college students (12,345 men and 7,968 women in sixty-five colleges) to the data obtained in 1966 for four-year college students, along with some data for samples of employed adults. These additions made the classification more comprehensive and reliable. Occupations were assigned to classes exactly as before; that is, mean VPI scores of all students aspiring to an occupation indicated that occupation's place in the classification.

In earlier classifications, the ordering of major classes and the arrangement of subgroups within major classes had no special meaning. In this study, however, the major classes and subclasses were arranged according to the hexagonal model in Figure 3. The hexagonal model was discovered when it was noticed that the intercorrelational matrix for the VPI scales used in the classification can be approximated by the distances within a hexagon. The data in Figure 3 are for a sample of 1,234 out of 12,345 male two-year college students in sixty-five colleges. The numbers in the figure are the correlations between the categories. A sample of 796 out of 7,968 females in the same colleges produced similar results.

This geometric model arranges student occupational aspirations according to their psychological relatedness, thereby making the classification more useful for vocational guidance and research in careers. In the hexagonal model the main categories are arranged in the following order—realistic, investigative, artistic, social, enterprising, and conventional (proceeding around the hexagon in a clockwise direction)—so that adjacent categories are most closely related. In general, close relationships are represented by short distances on the hexagon.

Using Figure 3 as a model, we can apply the same principle of arrangement to the subclasses within a major category by observing the following rule: Within a major category, arrange the subclasses so that the second and third code letters follow in clockwise order starting from the major category's first code. Thus the order within the realistic category is RI, RA, RS, RE, RC, and the order within the realistic-investigative subclass is RIA, RIS, RIE, and so on.

Intermediate classification. The goals of this intermediate form of the classification were to extend the classification to all common occupations in the United States and to arrange each subclass of occupations in order of level of general educational development (GED). The assignment of GED levels to occupations was, with few exceptions, a clerical task. Using the U.S. Department of Labor *Dictionary of Occupational Titles* (1965), occupations were assigned GED levels (1 through 6) according to their six-digit occupational code.

The ideal way to increase the comprehensiveness of the classification could have been to administer the VPI to large representative samples of employed adults, calculate mean VPI profiles, and assign occupations to the classification according to profile patterns. Because this expensive data collection was not possible, other alternatives were sought. The following paragraphs describe how data from divergent sources were translated from other systems or scales into the six classes represented by the VPI.

Campbell (1971) created six Vocational Preference Inventory scales for the Strong Vocational Interest Blank (SVIB). He accomplished this task by using the definitions of the personality types and lists of occupational titles given in Holland (1966b). Campbell's VPI scales provide an alternate form of the VPI. His brief scales, composed largely of occupational titles in the Strong, are similar to corresponding scales in the VPI. They contain many overlapping items, same or similar occupational titles, or related activity items. Campbell rescored some of the Strong criterion groups of employed adults with his alternate form of the VPI and produced VPI profiles for samples of students and employed adults. (For a complete account, see Campbell and Holland, 1972, or Campbell, 1971.)

For a sample of 76 occupations, the Campbell form of the VPI and the sixth revision of the VPI (Holland, 1965) agreed on the main classification of an occupation (one of the six categories) about 84 percent of the time. The next two letters in an occupational profile were rarely identical, but the majority of the occupations in question received the same combination of three highest letters of VPI scales. Parenthetically, the convergence of the VPI profiles obtained from the SVIB and the VPI profiles from other sources (Holland *et al.*, 1969) is of marked value, because that convergence (84 percent) reveals that aspirants for particular occupations resemble the employed adults in the same occupations.

The most sustained, scientific attempt to organize our knowledge of work activities is that of McCormick and his colleagues. Their contribution is not easily summarized because of its long time span, scope, and complexity. Their more recent work has been summarized by McCormick, Jeanneret, and Mecham (1969) and by McCormick, Jeanneret and Mecham (1972). McCormick, Jeanneret, and Mecham (1969) developed the Position Analysis Questionnaire as a method for assessing jobs directly. This comprehensive questionnaire contains 189 job elements intended to characterize the human behavior required in different jobs.

Data based on the Position Analysis Questionnaire have been used (1) for deriving estimates of the human attributes (aptitudes, interests, physical capacities, and so on) that a job requires, and (2) as the basis for identifying job dimensions. Mecham and McCormick (1969a) developed the attribute requirements (68) for the job elements (178) in the PAQ. In short, they used PAQ descriptions of individual jobs as data for deriving estimates of the human characteristics needed to perform those jobs. To accomplish this task, 68 attributes were selected as relevant to different kinds of work performance. Raters estimated the relevance of each attribute to the elements of the PAQ.

Median attribute ratings were derived and their reliabilities were estimated (most of these were in the .80s and .90s). This estimation of the attribute requirements from the PAQ means that it may be possible to establish useful job requirements using only job analysis data; that is, the usual situational validation of predictors might be ignored. In a related study, Mecham and McCormick (1969b) used the PAQ to estimate the attribute requirements of jobs, and validated these synthetic estimates against data based on the General Aptitude Test Battery (GATB) of the U.S. Employment Service. The results clearly indicate that the PAQ (a comprehensive job analysis) can be used to estimate the aptitudes that jobs require.

Finally, Jeanneret and McCormick (1969) investigated the hypothesis that there is "some structure underlying the domain of human work." Using 536 job analyses obtained by the PAQ, they performed principal component analyses of PAQ items that resulted in 5 overall factors and 27 divisional job dimensions. The divisional dimensions resulted from independent factor analyses of each of the major divisions of the PAQ. They also performed factor analyses of the PAQ item attribute profiles developed by Mecham and McCormick (1969a). The six independent analyses produced 21 divisional dimensions. Generally, the job dimensions obtained from job analyses and from attribute profiles appear sensible and consistent with one another as well as with the related literature.

McCormick, Mecham, and Jeanneret provided the author with the fruits of their work (called the Purdue data): 32 factor scores in standard score form for a sample of 879 occupations, including 5 overall factor scores and 27 factor scores resulting from factor analyses of the job elements within each of the six subdivisions of the PAQ (Jeanneret and McCormick, 1969; or Jeanneret and McCormick, 1972). The Purdue data were used for two purposes: (1) To determine the relationship between the Holland classification and the Purdue job factors, and (2) to extend the Holland classification to more occupations.

The first task was accomplished in this way: The Purdue jobs (832 of 879) were classified into the Holland categories. Forty-seven jobs were not classifiable, mainly because they had unusual occupational titles that could not be located in the DOT. These were eliminated from further consideration. Independent classifications of the remaining 832 Purdue jobs by two people resulted in 80 percent agreement; the other 20 percent were resolved by discussion.

A simple analysis of variance across five Holland occupational classes was performed for each of the 32 Purdue factors (the artistic class was omitted because the Purdue data contained only two artistic jobs). The results of this analysis are shown in Table 8, which gives the mean and standard deviation for each Purdue occupational dimension for the occupations classified as realistic, social, and so on.

The results in Table 8 are significant—all F tests are beyond the .001 level except two—and the implied relationships between Holland classes and Purdue factors are usually sensible and expected (see Jeanneret and McCormick, 1969,

TABLE 8

*Relation of Holland Classification (Occupational Categories)
to the Purdue Factored Dimension Scores for 832 Occupations*

Purdue Occupational Dimension		Holland Classification					
		Real	*Inv*	*Soc*	*Conv*	*Ent*	*F*
JD 19. Staff-	X	−.06	.81	.40	.09	−.56	22.20
related activities	SD	.68	1.45	1.01	.88	1.36	
JE 22. Unpleasant hazardous	X	.38	−.48	−.32	−.53	−.31	50.78
physical environment	SD	1.09	.36	.44	−.42	.55	
*JE 23. Personally demanding	X	.42	−.51	−1.20	.26	−1.17	148.58
situations (-social)	SD	.54	.96	1.47	.61	1.04	
JF 26. Unstructured vs. structured	X	−.20	.62	.63	−.31	.75	44.83
work	SD	.96	.73	.76	.87	.64	
JF 25. Attentive-discriminating	X	.06	.66	−.19	−.32	.27	11.38
work demands	SD	1.09	1.02	.97	.94	.89	
*JF 24. Businesslike work	X	.55	−.60	−.16	−.63	−1.01	168.62
situations (realistic)	SD	.64	.71	.94	.72	.72	
JF 27. Variable vs. regular	X	.18	−.43	−.12	−.37	.05	13.31
work schedule	SD	1.12	.62	.81	.66	.96	
JO 1. Decision-communication-	X	−.40	.87	.76	−.30	1.45	198.01
social responsibilities	SD	.64	.60	.92	.60	.82	
*JO 2. Skilled activities	X	.30	.85	−.42	−.47	−.39	45.14
(investigative)	SD	1.07	.80	.70	.47	.59	
JO 3. Physical activities and	X	−.24	.45	−.10	.44	.19	22.97
related environment conditions	SD	1.08	.60	.69	.60	.67	
JO 5. Information-processing	X	.40	−.58	−.09	−.86	.08	85.93
activities	SD	.84	.80	.77	.88	.64	
JO 4. Equipment-vehicle	X	.16	−.14	−.07	−.33	−.06	10.05
operation	SD	1.12	.73	.59	.51	.68	
JA 2. Perceptual interpre-	X	.10	.52	.11	−.24	−.30	9.71
tation	SD	1.03	1.15	1.08	.72	.67	
JB 8. Decision-making	X	−.24	1.09	.26	−.33	1.20	91.51
	SD	.84	.64	.91	.72	.78	
JB 9. Information-processing	X	−.47	.85	.38	.78	.03	87.01
	SD	.79	1.04	1.05	.89	.82	
JC 10. Machine-process	X	.34	.05	−.37	−.36	−.51	36.36
control	SD	1.04	.89	.58	.67	.65	
JC 14. Handling-manipulating	X	.19	−.49	−.01	.08	−.79	25.29
activities	SD	1.02	1.03	.94	.75	.79	
JC 12. Control-equipment	X	−.15	.26	.36	.17	.03	7.35
operation	SD	1.27	.45	.52	.54	.59	
JC 16. Skilled-technical	X	.08	−1.26	−.29	.30	−.27	25.82
activities	SD	1.10	1.20	.88	.54	.65	
*JC 15. Use of finger device	X	.34	−.39	.15	−.87	.11	70.62
vs. physical work (-conv.)	SD	.83	.84	.65	1.10	.58	
JC 11. Manual control-	X	−.31	−.02	.43	.36	.35	29.23
coordinated activities	SD	1.14	.97	.57	.49	.46	
JC 13. General body	X	−.07	.12	−.22	.20	.10	4.14
activity	SD	1.13	.82	.99	.62	.63	
*JD 17. Communication of	X	−.41	.71	.76	−.30	1.55	219.98
decisions-judgments (ent.)	SD	.48	.65	.97	.66	1.05	
JD 18. Job-related informa-	X	−.36	.22	−.03	.59	.49	47.16
tion exchange	SD	.76	1.02	.95	.97	1.19	

TABLE 8 (Continued)

Purdue Occupational Dimension		Holland Classification					
		Real	Inv	Soc	Conv	Ent	F
JD 21. Public-related	X	−.11	.28	−.05	.37	−.20	11.48
contact	SD	.86	.80	.88	.84	1.24	
JD 20. Supervisor-subordinate	X	−.16	−.14	.09	.22	.25	7.97
relationships	SD	.93	.77	.97	.93	1.13	
JA 3. Information from	X	−.50	.82	.75	.15	1.12	130.49
people	SD	.82	.66	.85	.65	.78	
JA 4. Visual input from	X	−.20	.26	.06	.36	.06	13.31
distal sources	SD	1.08	.55	.86	.66	.75	
JA 1. Visual input from	X	.31	.42	−.40	−.48	−.33	39.74
devices-materials	SD	1.04	.82	.68	.54	.67	
JA 5. Evaluation of information	X	−.01	.20	−.43	.31	−.17	11.19
from physical sources	SD	1.08	.80	.85	.41	1.01	
JA 6. Environmental awareness	X	.11	.37	−.33	−.15	−.04	6.26
	SD	1.04	1.28	.87	.76	1.08	
JA 7. Awareness of body	X	−.02	.08	−.25	.16	−.05	2.88
movement posture	SD	1.07	1.27	1.09	.64	.91	

*Purdue factors selected to create VPI profiles to add more occupations to Holland classification.
Note: For a complete account of the meaning of the Purdue Dimension scores, see Jeanneret and McCormick (1969) or McCormick, Jeanneret and Mecham (1972). The JO dimensions resulted from an overall components analysis of the Position Analysis Questionnaire, while dimensions labeled JA 1 through JF 27 resulted from separate analyses of each division in the PAQ. $F_{001} = 4.62$.
Source: Holland, J. L., Viernstein, M. C., Kuo, H., Karweit, N. L., and Blum, Z. D., A psychological classification of occupations. *Journal Supplement Abstract Service*, 1972, 2, 84.

and Holland, 1966b, for complete explanations of the concepts in this table). The evidence in Table 8 demonstrates that the Holland classification, developed almost entirely from psychological data, also encompasses more objective, situational data about jobs. Conversely, the Purdue factors encompass the Holland classification.

The second task was to use the Purdue data to create VPI profiles so that more occupations could be added to the Holland classification. Using Table 8, five Purdue factors were selected to represent the corresponding VPI scales and their associated occupational classes. These factors are identified with asterisks in Table 8. To obtain five-variable VPI profiles for each of the 832 jobs, a computer was programed to create a five-letter profile ranging from the highest to lowest standard score using the five Purdue factors. About 54 percent of the profiles had their peak or high point in agreement with their subjective classification obtained earlier. The errors of classification appeared plausible although large in number (46 percent); that is, if an occupation was misclassified, it was usually misclassified in an adjacent rather than distant category.

The final task was to integrate the data obtained from the Campbell form of the VPI using Strong data, the data from the Purdue factors, and the data from the testing of employed adults or occupational aspirants with the VPI. The data for each occupation were put on a card that showed the VPI profile, the number of subjects, the occupational title, and the source of data. Each occupation was represented by 1 to 42 cards, and the cards were collated by occupation.

To produce a single profile for an occupation, a variety of numerical, clerical, and artistic strategies were used. They included: (1) Counting the number of times a particular VPI letter or code occurred in the first, the second, or the third place in various profiles obtained from different sources and samples; (2) weighting subjectively the reliability and validity of one data source versus another; and (3) evaluating divergent profiles, particularly so that the data for men and women would be considered. In most cases, simple counting procedures were sufficient to arrive at a single profile. In general, divergences were not great, and resolutions of discrepancies were tied closely to the data. Appendix D illustrates the degree of convergence or divergence obtained by the use of VPI, Purdue, and Strong data.

A review of the 1960 census (Priebe, 1968) revealed that this intermediate classification contained all but 31 of the common occupations in the United States (50,000+). This deficiency was alleviated by estimating three-letter VPI profiles for the 31 occupations and adding them to the classification. This artistic process was performed by estimating which of the classified occupations these new occupations resembled. Because DOT codes provide estimates of the data, people, and things competencies demanded by an occupation, the values of these variables for occupations without empirically estimated VPI profiles could be compared with the DOT patterns of the various subclasses in the present classification. In this way, the validity of an occupation's proposed classification could be examined.

Current classification. The classification presented in Appendix B is the current revision of the classification. It differs in minor ways from the intermediate classification. An attempt was made to locate new VPI data for people in any occupation. These data were profiled for individual occupations and used to verify or revise the intermediate classification. A total of 21 changes were made. Of these, only 5 were changes of the first letter in an occupational code. In addition, occupations were added to clarify the meaning of small subcategories by adding a few related occupations and to make the classification more comprehensive. These additions were performed by using Viernstein's tables (1972) for extending the classification to all occupations in the Dictionary of Occupational Titles. Appendix E contains these tables so that a user can move from Holland to DOT code or vice-versa.

Validation

There are several kinds of evidence for the usefulness of the classification and the validity of its categories: (1) The evidence for the validity of the types reviewed earlier is also evidence for the validity of the categories and subcategories in the classification, since the VPI scales have been used to define both types *and* occupational categories. (2) The efficiency with which the classification orders occupational aspirations, work histories, or identifies current status of an individual occupation is another index of usefulness. And (3) the degree of fit between the hexagonal model and the data for a wide range of subjects assessed with diverse measures form another kind of evidence.

Categories. The purpose of the following studies was to show that the classification organizes occupations or people into homogeneous groups. If the classification performs this task well, people in the same category should possess similar personal traits, competencies, and interests, and they should possess similar aspirational or work histories; that is, they should move among the same or closely related categories. It is assumed that the higher the predictive validity of the classification, the more the classification organizes changes or moves among occupational aspirations or jobs.

Numerous studies show that people or occupations belonging to the same category have similar characteristics. Holland (1968b) found that people categorized as types have similar interests, self-ratings, life goals, competencies, personal traits, and attitudes. The relationships between the Holland categories and the diverse occupational dimensions developed by McCormick *et al.* (1969) also suggest that people in the same category have similar characteristics.

Campbell's (1971) listing of 202 occupations according to their mean score on the VPI scales (alternate form based on Strong items) is vivid evidence that the scales defining the categories organize occupations in terms of their similarity (see Campbell, 1971, E10-E15, pages 464-469). For example, the ten highest occupations on the realistic scale are machinists, tool and die makers, vocational agriculture teachers, skilled tradesmen, highway patrolmen, electricians, farmers, carpenters, policemen, and foresters. The high-scoring occupations on the remaining five scales display similar homogeneity.

Other studies of single occupations produce VPI codes that resemble or are identical with the codes assigned to the same occupation in the intermediate or current revision of the classification (Guzman, 1963; Jary, 1971; Schuldt and Stahmann, 1971; Stahmann, Osborn, and Williams, 1971). And Frantz (1969a, 1969b) has shown that the undergraduate and graduate fields of student personnel workers predict their current category of work. When the fields of study are assigned to main categories, the resulting percentages form an occupational profile of SEA for both their undergraduate and graduate fields. SEA is the code for counselors in the current classification.

Longitudinal tests of the classification have always been at least moderately successful. Holland and Whitney (1968) applied the classification to longitudinal data and obtained unusually efficient predictions of vocational aspirations over an eight- to twelve-month interval. For example, 79 percent of the men and 93 percent of the women reported successive vocational choices that were described as the same or related. Another analysis of the same data (Holland and Lutz, 1968) revealed that the predictive validity of a student's expressed choice was about twice that of the VPI when student choices were organized according to a preliminary form of the classification. In an unpublished analysis of Project Talent data, Claudy (personal communication, 1970) found that the category of a student's occupational choice in the 12th grade was a moderately efficient predictor of the category of his job five years later. And Bartlett (1970) performed similar analyses for predicting between the 9th and 10th (N = 143), 10th and 11th (N = 143), and 11th and 12th (N = 143) grades and obtained moderate to efficient predictions using only the six main categories to organize student occupational aspirations.

In a recent study of college graduates, Lucy (in press) found statistically significant and strong positive relationships between the category of a student's major field and the category of his current occupation using Holland's classification. Contingency coefficients for 6 X 6 tables range from .64 for a twenty-five-year interval to .74 for a fifteen-year interval. These are impressive findings, since Lucy's study spanned time intervals of ten to thirty-five years (803 alumni from the classes of 1935, 1940, 1945, 1950, 1955, and 1960).

Holland, Sorensen, Clark, Nafziger, and Blum (1973) applied the intermediate form of the classification to a national sample of retrospective work histories (N = 973) to test the predictive efficiency of the classification and related hypotheses from Holland's theory of careers. Analyses were performed by organizing and reorganizing the work histories according to the classification.

The classification appears to order lower-level occupational histories in an efficient way, well beyond chance. Over five- and ten-year intervals, 6 X 6 tables show that the percentages of people remaining in the same main categories are 77.3 and 74.2. Other analyses imply that all three letters in an occupational code have predictive validity. Still other hypotheses from the theory reveal that the "consistency" of a man's initial occupational code forecasts both his level of achievement and his tendency to change occupational categories. Last, a man's level of education, income, and prestige is predictable from his initial occupational code in accordance with the hypotheses about education and vocational achievement. All such analyses were statistically significant and usually substantial in size.

The positive results of this study are consistent with similar studies. Parsons (1971) has recently shown that the application of the classification to the work histories of a representative national sample of older men (N = 5,000, aged 45 to 59) also produces moderately efficient predictions. In a study of a representative national sample of young men (N = 5,000, aged 14 to 24), Nafziger, Holland, Helms, and McPartland (1972) found that 69 percent of the whites and 82 percent of the blacks remained in the same category over a two-year period. In another analysis, the authors report that the GED levels, used in the Holland classification, correlate .82 with the Duncan Socio-economic Index (N = 4,035).

Taken together, the application of the classification to both representative and unrepresentative populations has yielded relatively homogeneous groups that behave according to theoretical expectations, and the results are large enough to be of practical value.

Hexagonal arrangement. Since the discovery of the hexagonal model as a plan for interpreting the relationships among types, more evidence has been obtained to document the usefulness of the model.

Cole and her colleagues have shown that the hexagonal model can be used to map occupations in a single plane (Cole, Whitney, and Holland, 1971). They show that this spatial configuration can be used to estimate the degree of similarity between jobs, the congruence between a person and a prospective job, the degree of change involved in moving from one job to the next, and the differentiation of a person's interests. In related articles, Cole and Cole (1970) show how to create spatial configurations in a single plane, and Cole and Hanson (1971) demonstrate that the hexagonal model is a useful way to organize the relationships among the scales of the SVIB, the Kuder Occupational Interest Survey, the VPI, the Minnesota Vocational Interest Inventory (MVII), and the American College Testing Vocational Interest Profile (ACT VIP) for samples of men. The configurations of the scales for each of these inventories are similar and conform to the configuration of interest suggested by the hexagonal model. Likewise, Roe's (1956) circular ordering of interest groups proposed earlier is similar if not identical with the model.

In a recent study, Cole (1972) has shown that the circular structure of interests found for men also holds for women. In addition, when men and women are found in the same occupation, they occupy "similar positions within the structure." Consequently, if a woman's interests can be located in this structure, then the occupational data for both men and women can be used to orient women toward occupations—usually more occupations, since the data for women are limited to only a few occupations.

Crabtree (1971) assessed samples of high school students (759 boys and 672 girls) with the VPI and applied Cole's configural analyses to the matrixes of correlations for the VPI scales. He obtained configurations for boys and girls that were identical to earlier configurations (Holland *et al.*, 1969) in their ordering (RIASEC). In addition, Crabtree correlated the expected size of the correlations (from high to low) for every pair of scale combinations on the hexagon with the obtained correlations. For boys, *rho* equaled .86 (P < .01); for girls, *rho* equaled .74 (P < .01).

Using a sample of college freshmen who had taken the Self-directed Search, Edwards and Whitney (1972) also replicated Cole's planar results. Again, the ordering of scales was similar to earlier results. More important, they found separate and similar configurations for scales composed entirely of activities, competencies, occupations, and self-ratings:

> When the data are arranged according to the hexagonal model (10 hexagons), the average correlation for the three distances within each hexagon are as predicted 10 of 10 times. The correlations around the perimeter have the highest average; the correlations between every other type are lower; and the three correlations between opposite types have the lowest average correlation.

NEW RESEARCH NEEDS

The review of the evidence supports the main hypotheses of the theory. The types appear to grow up, perceive occupations, search for occupations, move among occupations, and behave according to theoretical expectations. The environmental models appear useful to characterize educational and occupational environments. Of special importance, the environmental definitions, based only on a census of types, appear to incorporate many physical and nonpsychological aspects of an environment. And, to a limited degree, types are influenced by environments as predicted. Finally, the classification receives strong support: (1) It has been extended to all occupations in the DOT; (2) it has substantial long-term validity for representative and unrepresentative samples of adolescents and adults; and (3) the hexagonal arrangement of the classification has been found to be a useful model for structuring interest inventories, self-ratings, competencies, and activities.

These tests of earlier versions of the theory, however, have revealed a clear group of weaknesses. The formulations for the types have often been too ambiguous to test with clear results. The characteristics attributed to types often overlap from type to type or show only trivial differences. The hypotheses about consistency and homogeneity (differentiation) receive only mixed support, although the large-scale analytical studies have usually been positive. The tests of the environmental hypotheses in research imply that other environmental forces must be dealt with—especially size, complexity, and power. In short, a census of types is not sufficient to cope with all environmental influences. Finally, occupations in the classification tend to shift categories, depending upon the population used to define an occupation's category. Normally, these shifts are minor, but they still undermine the stability of the system.

The weaknesses of the theory in the past are due largely to the weaknesses of the early theory itself, in which statements did not always lend themselves to explicit tests because the formulations were sometimes vague and confusing. The present statement should encourage more explicit and analytical tests of all hypotheses. The structure of the types, the environments, and their interactions are now simpler, clearer, and articulated by an explicit calculus—the hexagonal model.

The most acute needs for new research seem to be: (1) More comprehensive studies of the environmental hypotheses. Although Astin and Richards have performed useful pioneering work, this difficult area has attracted few investigators. (2) More analytical studies of person-environment interactions. The restatement of the theory makes it possible to examine interactions more analytically and comprehensively. Within such studies, we need to acquire a clearer knowledge of the process of change. Although the theory has been useful for coping with the stability of vocational choice, its ability to cope with change has been weak. The new hypotheses about the process of change may be helpful in initiating such studies.

The importance of understanding change in behavior cannot be overestimated. If we develop a good working knowledge of change, a host of practical and potent applications become possible. They include how to design more effective guidance devices and systems, how to foster more satisfying vocational decisions, how to redesign jobs for greater personal fulfillment, and how to manipulate others for a variety of socially desirable purposes.

Studies of the types appear to be of secondary importance, although there is a clear need to learn whether the new formulations are more useful than the old. Presumably, they should lead to less overlap among types and generally to clearer results. More analytical studies of these formulations are also needed. The hypotheses about development appear promising, but personal development is a psychological jungle. Researchers should approach it with full warning of the swamps and uncharted pitfalls.

Studies of the classification also seem secondary. The classification has survived some severe tests of its usefulness. Now it needs a long and probably interminable series of minor revisions and tests to answer questions like the following: Does the SDS provide a better definition of the classification than the VPI? What should the place of any new occupation be? Have all the occupations classified so far been accurately classified? These and other questions usually require enormous amounts of data and other resources. Equally troublesome, there are few rewards for the execution of this much-needed practical engineering activity.

To supplement this outline for new work, I have included "Some Research Suggestions for Students" as Appendix F to provide a convenient way to influence research, to help students, and to say some things I have been wanting to say for a long time.

SUMMARY

The evidence for the usefulness of the theory and its classification scheme is extensive and typically positive. Positive support was obtained in the majority of studies of children, adolescents, and adults of both sexes. It is assumed that the present revision of the theory will produce more positive results, since the present statement is more explicit and more clearly structured than earlier attempts.

Practical Applications

chapter 6

The purpose of this chapter is to outline with examples the main practical applications of the theory to vocational guidance, social science, personnel work, vocational education, and higher education. These applications are usually offered in explicit fashion for three reasons: (1) Readers rarely have the time or the inclination to spell out theoretical implications. (2) Practical applications are a rich source of ideas for revision. Most important, (3) theories should have something useful to say about the conduct of practical affairs.

VOCATIONAL GUIDANCE

The goal of vocational guidance—matching men and jobs—remains the same despite much talk, research, and speculation. Our devices, techniques, classifications, and theories are more comprehensive and sophisticated than in the days of Parsons (1909), the founder of vocational guidance, but the goal is still one of helping people find jobs that they can do well and that are fulfilling.

Perhaps the only radical shift in point of view is the belief that it is valuable to see the processes of vocational decisions (vocational choice, choice of training, and work history) in the context of a person's development. This view has led to more activities planned to improve the quality of a person's decision-making and knowledge of self and the occupational world, but the main test of this reorientation also lies in a more felicitous accommodation of men and jobs. So far, this eminently plausible point of view has failed to produce effective practical mechanisms for improving vocational decision-making; most vocational guidance programs in schools and elsewhere remain a hodgepodge of pragmatic, artistic, atheoretical practices and devices. They differ largely in expense rather than in effectiveness—the larger the budget, the larger the collection of materials, practices, and staff.

The present theory, with its occupational classification and related instruments, offers many practical applications for vocational guidance. The theory and its instruments can be used to (1) organize occupational information in simple, clear-cut, usable terms; (2) explain and interpret both vocational data and vocational behavior; and (3) provide specific formulations to facilitate vocational development and help those people whose vocational development has gone awry.

Organization

The organization of information is a major problem in the practice of vocational guidance. Information about occupations comes in many forms that are difficult to integrate intellectually: brochures, rule-of-thumb classifications, lists of local occupations, complex and exhaustive classifications (DOT), single file drawers of material, whole filing cabinets of data, and even huge collections for which librarians are needed. In addition, the assessment of students or adults produces highly specific information that, if organized at all, is often organized in idiosyncratic and unexamined ways.

The present classification provides a simple method for organizing occupational information that is easily comprehensible by both clients and counselors, but that still allows for the complexity of occupations. The classification has undergone numerous positive tests, and its theoretical origin and construction ensure its continued revision and flexibility.

The organization of all occupational information in a single system would make the information more accessible and more easily understood, and should reduce the number of personnel (such as special librarians or clerical workers) involved in maintaining such materials. Clients could use occupational materials almost as easily as counselors and would no longer have to be led through ad hoc occupational files and libraries. This change in role for the client should encourage his independence and free counselors for more complex and appropriate activities.

The organization of assessment data according to the classification should also be advantageous. Counselors can use the typological formulations of the theory to organize the data they obtain from interviews, records, and aptitude and interest devices.

The development of the Self-directed Search (Holland, 1970) illustrates one way in which the classification and the theory have been used to organize the assessment of the person and the world of occupations within the same framework. The assessment booklet provides a simple way for the person to determine his resemblance to each of the six personality types, and the occupational classification booklet provides an "occupational file" in the same terms (six types of occupations), so that the person can search for occupations that correspond to his personality pattern. Without such a classification and its associated theory, it is not possible to organize both personal and occupational data and to explicitly integrate these divergent kinds of information.

Seen another way, the SDS simulates in an explicit way what counselors, parents, psychologists, and personnel workers do in more intuitive and less precise ways. For example, vocational counselors usually obtain aptitude, interest, and personality data by divergent methods that have poorly formulated and often unrelated rationales. Using their best judgment, they attempt a formulation about a person (analogous to the summary code of the SDS). Then they attempt to determine what occupations go with the formulation. This task is especially hazardous for three reasons: (1) The formulation for the person usually lacks a clear and examined rationale; (2) the classification scheme usually lacks a clear and examined rationale; and (3) the translation from person to occupation is made even more difficult, since the formulations do not share the same concepts and frequently no empirical tests have been made of the validity of the method of translation.

The classification can, in principle, be used to organize most of the components in an entire vocational guidance program. For example:

1. The assessment of clients can be done with the Vocational
   Preference Inventory (Holland, 1965), the Self-directed
   Search (Holland, 1970), or the Holland Scales for the Strong
   Vocational Interest Blank (Campbell and Holland, 1972), which
   yield scores and profiles in terms of the personality types.
   Other inventories can be used (such as the Kuder Preference
   Record), but their adaptation would require some additional
   research.
2. All data on client characteristics from interviews, tests, reports,
   and biographical questionnaires can be organized and stored
   within the framework of the theory's typology.
3. Career literature, employer announcements, and listings of
   vacant positions can all be organized and filed in a system that
   uses the classification. This would be more helpful and
   meaningful to clients than storing these items on the usual
   alphabetical or chronological basis, because it would
   immediately identify them in terms of related occupations, abilities
   required, and so on. It would also help counselors to locate and
   remedy any deficiencies that they may not have noticed when
   they were collecting these materials in the first place—for
   example, lack of information about artistic or social job
   opportunities would be apparent.
4. The theory should allow counselors to prepare occupational
   information programs that are reasonably representative of the

world of work. The classification of occupations can be used to organize classroom projects, lectures by outside speakers, film programs, visits to places of employment, interviews with former students who have gone on to various types of work, and even trial job experiences. Hoppock (1968) has given details of the many ways in which occupational information can be presented, but the Holland theory can be used with any method of presentation to ensure that the content of programs is not unbalanced. For example, if a program of visits is being planned, the person organizing it might arrange for his students to make at least one visit to observe a job in each of the six major categories of the occupational classification.

5. Information about college courses and vocational training opportunities can also be organized and filed on the basis of the Holland theory. In particular, colleges can be classified by using the Environmental Assessment Technique (EAT) (Astin and Holland, 1961; Astin, 1963); which employs the six Holland categories to characterize educational institutions.

Explanation

The theory and its classification can also be used to explain and interpret vocational data and vocational behavior. Despite their current low status among practitioners, diagnostic activities play a large role in vocational counseling. Students, adults, and parents want to know what tests mean and what their personal values and competencies mean occupationally. They voice many other queries that call for valid assessments and reliable forecasts.

The theory and its classification possess some explanatory possibilities for coping with common diagnostic problems in vocational practice. The typological formulations can be used to interpret interest inventories, to clarify the divergent occupational choices of people in conflict, to interpret work histories, to predict the outcomes of proposed person-environment interactions, to explain the origins of interests, and to explain the occurrence of adaptive and maladaptive vocational development. And of equal or greater importance, the theory implies remedial actions or treatments for facilitating more adaptive vocational behavior. These ideas are elaborated in the following paragraphs.

Because most interest inventories have only a perfunctory rationale, they can benefit from the application of the theory. Table 1 indicates what interest inventory scores are estimates of what types. Using the typology, counselors are able to (1) interpret individual interest scores according to the formulations, (2) predict what categories of occupations appear congruent for a person, (3) estimate the consistency and differentiation of a person's profile, and (4) estimate the consistency between a person's current choice and his interest inventory profile. Needless to say, counselors perform these activities now in one way or another. The contribution of the theory is to provide more explicit, comprehensive, and reliable rules for conducting them. To illustrate, Frantz (1972) has developed a simple method for rescoring the SVIB so that people with flat profiles could be more clearly differentiated and understood. Frantz uses the classification to rescore the occupational and field items in the SVIB. The rescoring method provides differentiated or nonflat profiles for the majority of subjects.

A person's conflicting occupational choices can be classified and examined for their special character and the psychological distance between them. Using the theory, a counselor can interpret a student's occupational conflict—a process that might aid both. For example, a boy trying to decide between mechanical engineering (RIE) and farming (RIE) should experience little conflict. A discussion of their psychological similarities might simplify his decision and suggest that other factors—such as style of life, capital, and special aptitudes—may help resolve this difficulty. In contrast, a girl trying to decide between medical technologist (ISA) and nurse (SIA) should profit from a discussion of the relative importance of I and S in these codes.

A client's work history or his history of occupational aspirations can be coded according to the classification and inspected for the degree of consistency. The coding can be done by the client or counselor and freely discussed. The client can also be asked to read portions of this book as a method of increasing self-understanding. And a person's successive occupational codes can be arranged in three columns (as in the SDS) and the code letters weighted 3, 2, and 1 so that a single summary can be obtained for his occupational history. This summary code can be then compared with test results, current aspirations, and occupational opportunities.

A person's SDS or VPI profile can be used to estimate the level of his vocational development or maturity. In the theory, a high level of maturity equals having a personality pattern characterized by high degrees of consistency and differentiation. Table 9 suggests a scoring system for SDS or VPI profiles in terms of levels of personal or vocational development.

In this scheme, persons at the higher levels should need only superficial assistance in vocational planning because they possess the personal characteristics that lead to better decisions. In contrast, persons at the lower levels of vocational development require more extensive help. According to the theory, maladaptive vocational development equals the failure to develop a consistent and differentiated personality pattern. In theoretical terms, maladaptive vocational development probably occurs in one of five major ways:

1. A person has had insufficient experience to acquire well-defined interests, competencies, or perceptions of himself.
2. A person has had insufficient experience to learn about the major kinds of occupational environments.

TABLE 9
A Diagnostic and Treatment Plan

Formulations	Diagnostic Signs	Treatment Programs
Information (self)		
Satisfactory	Consistent and well-defined	—
Lacks information	SDS profile vs. inconsistent	Experience
Has confusing informa-tion	and poorly defined SDS profile	Counseling
Information (environment)		
Satisfactory	Consistent and well-defined	—
Lacks information	VPI profile vs. inconsistent and poorly defined VPI	Computer-assisted informa-tion services, work, reading
Has conflicting informa-tion	profile	Counseling
Translation (interaction)		
Informed-uninformed (can make useful translations)	Consistency between occu-pational aspiration and SDS code	Self-directed Search, coun-seling
Degree of self-confidence	Add up self-ratings in SDS	Counseling, competence training
Alienation	Rare SDS codes	?
Complexity of outlook	Artistic minus realistic scale	Time
Rate of development	Degree of differentiation of SDS profile	Time

3. A person has had ambiguous or conflicting experience about his interests, his competencies, and his personal characteristics.
4. A person has acquired ambiguous and conflicting information about the major environments.
5. A person may suffer from none of these deficiencies, but may lack sufficient information about himself or confidence to translate personal characteristics into occupational opportunities. In addition, he may have a slow rate of development so that he is slow in developing a well-defined profile of interests and competencies; he may have a complex outlook so that he makes decisions slowly; or he may be alienated so that he is uninvolved or denies the need to choose.

When people are unable to resolve their own vocational decisions, a review of these five possibilities can be undertaken with the person's active participation. At one extreme, many young people would be expected to be deficient in all five ways. At the other extreme, most older people would be expected to be proficient in all five ways. In theoretical terms, psychological maturity and vocational maturity (Super, 1972; Crites, 1971) are similar concepts and are equivalent to freedom from the deficiencies outlined above. Contrary to popular opinion, students appear to suffer more from translation problems than from a lack of occupational information.

In contrast, adaptive vocational behavior is the outcome of the following events:

1. A person has had sufficient experience to develop well-defined interests and competencies.
2. A person has had sufficient experience to acquire a useful library of occupational stereotypes, especially in his area of interest.
3. A person has had sufficient self-clarifying experience so that his picture of his interests, his competencies, and his personal characteristics is accurate.
4. A person has had sufficient clarifying occupational experience so that his library of occupational information and stereotypes has a useful degree of validity and is free of major contradictions.
5. A person has sufficient self-confidence and cultural involvement to make vocational decisions as the need occurs.

Because most people have had these necessary developmental experiences and get along without formal vocational guidance services, we need to put substantial effort into creating conditions that lead to these outcomes and providing vocational assistance in more selective ways. For example, many people need only placement help, because they have all the other prerequisites for employment. We also need to make occupational information more accessible. It should be available in easily comprehensible form without appointments and without professional supervision, and in many places besides employment centers or counseling offices. At the same time, we need to make translation materials like the SDS more accessible so that the many people who need only superficial help can quickly receive what they need. The counseling resources can then be conserved for people with remedial or more complex requirements.

Remediation

The diagnostic techniques and formulations summarized earlier suggest some activities, methods, and ideas to facilitate vocational and personal development and to help people whose vocational development has gone awry. The five formulations listed (see page 89) in conjunction with a person's personality pattern (as assessed by the VPI or SDS) can be used to estimate a person's deficiencies or misunderstandings.

To illustrate, a person with a consistent and differentiated profile should be able to get along with minimal assistance—usually just educational and occupational information. A person with a grossly inconsistent and flat (undifferentiated) profile probably requires vocational counseling and perhaps psychotherapy to resolve some gross misperceptions of himself and the world.

Later, this kind of person may also require special experience (part-time work, reading, occupational experience kits) in order to acquire a more accurate knowledge of himself and the major kinds of work. Between these two extremes, it is important to determine the specific kinds of information, experience, or clarification that a client needs. The theory suggests that if a person has a well-defined profile, information is the principal need, whatever his age. The theory implies that if a person is young (age 15 to 20), or has an inconsistent or relatively flat profile, clarification or experience or both are the principal needs.

The search for these informational gaps or needed clarifications can be performed with the active cooperation of the client by reviewing the five diagnostic propositions. This activity could be performed in an interview or by a careful review of a person's responses to the SDS. Subsequently, an educational plan could be developed to help a person resolve his vocational decision by securing the necessary information, experience, or counseling.

These diagnostic and correlated treatment ideas can be applied to groups in several ways. Student SDS profiles could be sorted into two main groups—those with well-defined profiles and those with poorly defined profiles. Students with well-defined profiles could be given ready access to occupational, test, and other information. Students with poorly defined profiles could be seen individually to work out a plan of education or special assistance.

The distributions of SDS profiles for a school could be used to organize and distribute a school's counseling resources. In this approach, the idea is to provide information and experience that will foster the development of adaptive vocational behavior. Presumably, normal or adaptive personal development leads to a differentiated and consistent personality pattern. In general, the theory would suggest the following strategies:

1. Provide students with relevant school and nonschool experience. This means giving them the opportunity to experience the six curriculums *and* the six kinds of nonschool experiences. This orientation implies that unless schools, parents, or other agencies provide a full range of experience, they lessen a student's ability to understand himself and his future possibilities.
2. Provide students with accurate and accessible information about themselves and jobs over a long time span rather than at a few critical decision points.
3. Provide students with translations of personal characteristics and jobs that are readily accessible and easily comprehended. The typical use of tests violates this principle. Test information is usually inaccessible, not clearly translated, incomplete, and unintegrated with other data.

By establishing a coherent and integrated set of experiences and informative methods, schools should be able to reach most students. These preliminary diagnostic and treatment plans could be elaborated so that a number of special treatments would be available and effective for students who are at different stages of development or who have different requirements.

In addition, schools should create special programs or adopt only portions of standard programs to meet the typical needs of their student population. Because student needs for vocational assistance will vary according to distributions of student types and family economic background, standard programs in which everyone gets everything can be wasteful and ineffective.

The theory, the classification, and the diagnostic and treatment formulations should be useful in planning methods to accelerate adaptive vocational behavior in school and work settings. Until vocational counseling devotes more of its resources to the long-term encouragement of adaptive vocational behavior, practitioners will be inundated with remedial and emergency activities.

SOCIAL SCIENCE

Although the following list is not exhaustive, it illustrates some ways that the theory can be used to cope with common problems in social science. The reader can probably develop additional applications for his own special interests.

1. The theory can be used to form groups and subgroups to interpret the results of experiments or surveys or simplify the individual-differences treatment problem. For instance, Owens (1968), in modifying Cronbach's proposal (1957) for a single scientific discipline of psychology, stresses the need to group people according to their patterns of prior experience so that we can develop laws for different types and subtypes rather than going to either extreme—to studies of individuals or whole populations. The present typology is a practical method for this purpose.

2. The theory can be used to equate experimental and control groups according to personality patterns when true experiments are not possible. Depending upon the data and sample size, the social scientist can compare experimentals and controls of the same type only, compare experimentals and controls whose distributions of types are identical or not significantly different, or compare only experimentals and controls who have identical personality patterns—RSEs versus RSEs, and so on.

3. The theory can be applied in the experimental study of educational, social, and work groups. These might include studies of various typological

combinations and their outcomes: group productivity, satisfaction, learning, creative performance, personal development. For example, the typology provides a simple technique for creating groups ranging from extreme homogeneity (SEAs only) to extreme heterogeneity (equal numbers of each type).

4. The theory can be used in studies of work histories, occupational mobility, and census data. The reexamination of occupational data by classifying according to the theory appears to be one of its most promising applications. The classification will allow economists, psychologists, and sociologists to analyze occupational data in two major ways—according to personality pattern or kind of person and according to level of competence or talent. These differentiations are a simple way to avoid treating all people as interchangeable units, a common practice in economic and sociological research. Even the simple coding of existing tables of occupational data without any manipulation of the data is often useful for interpreting trends and relationships. For example, O'Shea and Harrington (1972) found the classification useful for interpreting their factor analyses of the Strong Vocational Interest Blank and the Occupational Interest Survey. When the scales in these inventories were assigned Holland three-letter codes, the similarities among factors became clear. This same procedure also facilitated the naming of factors.

The flexibility of the classification makes it possible to cope with both representative and unrepresentative populations. To illustrate, when the number of people or occupations in a main category is large, all three-letter subcategories of a main category can be used to analyze the data; when the number is small, only the main categories or the two-letter categories can be used. Studies by Holland et al. (1971) and Nafziger et al. (1972) illustrate how the classification can be contracted or expanded to deal with a skewed distribution of occupational data. Because a national representative sample has an abnormal distribution of types (R = 82 percent, I = 5 percent, A = 2 percent, S = 2 percent, E = 6 percent, C = 4 percent), Nafziger et al. (1972) used all the three-letter realistic categories for the realistic data, but used only single categories for the remaining data. In contrast, distributions of the occupational aspirations of college students will usually contain few realistic occupations, but many social and investigative occupations, and so on. Accordingly, the realistic categories can be contracted and the social and investigative categories expanded to deal with this nonrepresentative sample.

5. The theory is useful in comparative cultural studies. For example, Richards (1971) has shown that the application of the classification to Japanese universities yields results that closely resemble the results obtained from American universities. And Nafziger et al. (1972) have shown that the typology is helpful for understanding the differences between two subcultures (blacks and whites) in the United States. They show that the distributions of

types in national representative samples of men and women are different for blacks and whites; larger proportions of blacks are realistic types.

PERSONNEL WORK, VOCATIONAL EDUCATION, AND HIGHER EDUCATION

The applications cited for vocational guidance also apply to the areas of work and education, because vocational assessment and counseling are major functions in each. In addition, the theory has some specific applications to some of the other problems of personnel work, vocational education, and higher education.

Personnel Work

The classification may be particularly useful in two situations: First, in large organizations, in which problems of staff development, transfer, promotion, and personnel planning have to be solved by moving personnel from one function to another. For example, the classification can be used to organize and locate similar jobs for people who must be transferred; the classification can be used in personnel planning to compare the distribution of types needed in the future with the distribution of types currently employed. Second, in rapidly changing organizations where technological developments and altered objectives necessitate the creation of totally new jobs. In these situations, the classification has clear practical implications for recruitment and selection procedures, training programs, analysis and redesign of jobs, improvement of communication and cooperation within and between work groups, and the general formulation of personnel policies and practices. For instance, a person's SDS or VPI profile could be used to design a more satisfying job that would maximize his interests and competencies and minimize his aversions and deficiencies. Congenial work groups with more effective matching of superiors and employees might be obtained by taking advantage of individual personality patterns.

At a more macroscopic level, the classification provides a theoretical system for assessing the effects of national manpower recruiting and training policies. For instance, the census data could be converted to the present classification and studied longitudinally for the effects of economic, recruiting, and training policies. The problems of relocating and retraining realistic types, who form the main group and who are now being displaced by machines and higher educational requirements, could be examined in terms of the classification and the formulation for the realistic type.

Vocational Education

The classification implies six "curricular clusters" in secondary and technical schools or institutes, and the subcategories imply some ways to structure single clusters. Such clusters would demand consonant competencies and interests, and make teaching a more manageable and effective experience for both students and teachers. The classification links fields of training to occupational possibilities. In vocational education or "career education," the theory could be used to organize an entire school program: curricular clusters, vocational guidance and placement services, occupational exploration programs, and research evaluations. The clarity and content of the vocational education or career education missions make them especially amenable to use of the theory.

Higher Education

The classification implies a clustering or reorganization of curriculums in two- and four-year colleges. Whitney and Holland (1969) have proposed such a reorganization for colleges and outlined its advantages for students, faculty, and administrators. The authors believe that their six-cluster scheme would increase the similarity between teacher and student interests, encourage vocational exploration, and improve student learning and development. Independently, Conary (1969) has used the classification as a rationale for organizing a new two-year college into four institutes: (1) Institute of Applied Humanities (artistic types), (2) Institute of Business and Management (social-conventional and social-enterprising types), (3) Institute of Human Affairs (social-investigative and social-artistic types), and (4) Institute of Natural and Applied Sciences (realistic and investigative types). This particular plan appears to be working well. What we need now are some comprehensive evaluations of its virtues and deficiencies, and a few adventurous colleges to try out the proposal or some variation of it.

SUMMARY

The organizational, explanatory, and facilitative implications of the theory for vocational guidance have been outlined, and some of its applications for social science, personnel work, vocational education, and higher education have been examined. Within these broad areas, the theory seems most useful for vocational guidance. And the organizational functions, as opposed to the explanatory and facilitative functions, are assumed to be more explicit and more firmly grounded. In general, the practical applications need to be extended and verified in a greater variety of settings—clinical, educational and industrial.

References

ABE, C., & HOLLAND, J. L. A description of college freshmen: I. Students with different vocational choices. ACT Research Report No. 3. Iowa City: The American College Testing Program, 1965. (a)

———. A description of college freshmen: II. Students with different vocational choices. ACT Research Report No. 4. Iowa City: The American College Testing Program, 1965. (b)

ADLER, A. *Social interest*. New York: Putnam, 1939.

ANDREWS, H. A. Personality patterns and vocational choice: A test of Holland's theory with adult part-time community college students. Unpublished doctoral dissertation, University of Missouri, 1971.

APOSTAL, R. A. Personality type and preferred college subculture. *Journal of College Student Personnel*, 1970, **11**, 206-209.

———, & HARPER. P. Basic interests in personality. *Journal of Counseling Psychology*, 1972, **19**, 167-168.

ASTIN, A. W. Further validation of the environmental assessment technique. *Journal of Educational Psychology*, 1963, **54**, 217-226.

———. Distribution of students among higher educational institutions. *Journal of Educational Psychology*, 1964, **55**, 276-287.

———. College preferences of very able students. *College and University*, 1965, **40**, 282-297. (a)

———. Classroom environment in different fields of study. *Journal of Educational Psychology*, 1965, **56**, 275-282. (b)

———. Effect of different college environments on the vocational choices of high aptitude students. *Journal of Counseling Psychology*, 1965, **12**, 28-34. (c)

———. *Who goes where to college?* Chicago: Science Research Associates, 1965. (d)

———. *The college environment*. Washington, D.C.: American Council on Education, 1968.

———, & HOLLAND, J. L. The environmental assessment technique: A way to measure college environments. *Journal of Educational Psychology*, 1961, **52**, 308-316.

ASTIN, A. W., & PANOS, R. J. *The educational and vocational development of American college students*. Washington, D.C.: American Council on Education, 1969.

BAILEY, R. L. Testing Holland's theory. *Measurement and Evaluation in Guidance*, 1971, **4**, 108-114.

BAIRD, L. L. The relation of vocational interests to life goals, self-ratings of ability and personality traits, and potential for achievement. *Journal of Counseling Psychology*, 1970, **17**, 233-239.

BANDUCCI, R. Accuracy of stereotypic perceptions of types and levels of occupations in relation to background and personal characteristics of high school senior boys. Unpublished doctoral dissertation, University of Iowa, 1968.

BARCLAY, J. R. Approach to the measurement of teacher "press" in the secondary curriculum. *Journal of Counseling Psychology*, 1967, **14**, 552-567.

_____ . *A research manual for the Barclay Classroom Climate Inventory*. Lexington, Ky.: University of Kentucky, 1970

_____ . The influence of paternal occupation on social interaction measures in elementary school children. *Journal of Vocational Behavior*, 1972, **2**, 433-446.

BARKER, R. G., & GUMP, P. V. *Big school, small school.* Stanford, Calif.: Stanford University Press, 1964.

BARTLETT, W. E. Vocational choice stability matrix: Development, application, and implications. *Indiana Personnel and Guidance Journal*, 1970, Spring, 71-77.

BATES, G. L., PARKER, H. J., & McCOY, J. F. Vocational rehabilitants' personality and work adjustment: A test of Holland's theory of vocational choice. *Psychological Reports*, 1970, **26**, 511-516.

BELL, R. Q. A reinterpretation of the direction of effects in studies of socialization. *Psychological Review*, 1968, **75**, 81-95.

BLAKENEY, R. N., MATTESON, M. T., & HOLLAND, T. A. A research note on the new SVIB Holland scales. *Journal of Vocational Behavior*, 1972, **2**, 239-43.

BOHN, M. J., JR. Psychological needs related to vocational personality types. *Journal of Counseling Psychology*, 1966, **13**, 306-309.

BORDIN, E. S. A theory of interests as dynamic phenomena. *Educational and Psychological Measurement*, 1943, **3**, 49-66.

BORGEN, F. H., WEISS, D. J., TINSLEY, H. E., DAWIS, R. V., & LOFQUIST, L. H. *Occupational reinforcer patterns.* Bulletin 48. Minneapolis-Industrial Relations Center, University of Minnesota, 1968.

BROWN, R. D. Peer group influence in a college residence hall. Unpublished doctoral dissertation, University of Iowa, 1966.

BRUE, E. J. Characteristics of transfer and occupational students in community colleges: A comparative study. Unpublished doctoral dissertation, University of Iowa, 1969.

CAMPBELL, D. P. Comment. *Personnel and Guidance Journal*, 1968, **46**, 434-436.

_____ . *Handbook for the Strong vocational interest blank*. Stanford, Calif.: Stanford University Press, 1971.

_____ , & HOLLAND, J. L. Applying Holland's theory to Strong's data. *Journal of Vocational Behavior*, 1972, 2, 353-376.

CHANEY, F. B., & OWENS, W. A. Life history antecedents of sales research and general engineering interests. *Journal of Applied Psychology*, 1964, **48**, 101-105.

COCKRIEL, I. W. Some data concerning the Vocational Preference Inventory and the Strong Vocational Interest Blank. *Journal of Vocational Behavior*, 1972, 2, 251-254.

COLE, N. S. On measuring the vocational interests of women. ACT Research Report No. 49. Iowa City: The American College Testing Program, 1972.

_____, & COLE, J. W. L. An analysis of spatial configuration and its application to research in higher education. ACT Research Report No. 35. Iowa City: The American College Testing Program, 1970.

COLE, N. S., & HANSON, G. An analysis of the structure of vocational interests. ACT Research Report No. 40. Iowa City: The American College Testing Program, 1971.

COLE, N. S., WHITNEY, D. R., & HOLLAND, J. L. A spatial configuration of occupations. *Journal of Vocational Behavior*, 1971, 1, 1-9.

CONARY, F. M. An alternate approach to clustering. Research Advisory No. 5, Brookdale Community College, Lincroft, N.J., 1969.

CRABTREE, P. D. A test of Holland's hexagonal model of occupational classification using a rural high school population. Unpublished doctoral dissertation, Ohio University, 1971.

CRITES, J. O. The maturity of vocational attitudes in adolescence. *APGA Inquiry Series*, No. 2. Washington, D.C.: American Personnel and Guidance Association, 1971.

CRONBACH, L. J. The two disciplines of scientific psychology. *American Psychologist*, 1957, 12, 671-684.

CRUTCHFIELD, R. S., WOODWORTH, D. G., & ALBRECHT, R. E. Perceptual performance and the effective person. Personnel Laboratory, U.S. Air Force, ASTIA Document No. AD 151 039. Lackland Air Force Base, Texas, 1958.

DARLEY, J. G. A preliminary study of relations between attitude, adjustment, and vocational interest tests. *Journal of Educational Psychology*, 1938, 29, 467-473.

_____, & HAGENAH, T. *Vocational interest measurement.* Minneapolis: University of Minnesota Press, 1955.

DAYTON, C. M., & UHL, N. P. Relationship between Holland Vocational Preference Inventory scores and performance measures of high school students. Cooperative Project Research No. 5-0581-2-12-1. College Park, Md.: Research and Demonstration Center, University of Maryland, 1966.

DOLLIVER, R. H. Strong Vocational Interest Blank versus expressed vocational interests: A review. *Psychological Bulletin*, 1969, 72, 95-107.

EDWARDS, K. J., & WHITNEY, D. R. A structural analysis of Holland's personality types using factor and configural analysis. *Journal of Counseling Psychology*, 1972, 19, 136-145.

ELTON, C. F. Male career role and vocational choice: Their prediction with personality and aptitude variables. *Journal of Counseling Psychology*, 1967, 14, 99-105.

_____. The interaction of environment and personality: A test of Holland's theory. *Journal of Applied Psychology*, 1971, 55, 114-118.

_____, & ROSE, H. A. Male occupational constancy and change: Its prediction according to Holland's theory. *Journal of Counseling Psychology*, 1970, 17, Part 2, No. 6.

FOLSOM, C. H., JR. An investigation of Holland's theory of vocational choice. *Journal of Counseling Psychology*, 1969, **16**, 260-266.

———. The validity of Holland's theory of vocational choice. Unpublished doctoral dissertation, University of Maine, 1971.

FORER, B. R. A diagnostic interest blank. *Rorchach Research Exchange and Journal of Projective Techniques*, 1948, **12**, 1-11.

———. Personality dynamics and occupational choice. Paper presented at the American Psychological Association meetings, Chicago, 1951.

FORTNER, M. L. Vocational choices of high school girls: Can they be predicted? *Vocational Guidance Quarterly*, 1970, **19**, 203-206.

FRANTZ, T. T. Backgrounds of student personnel workers. *Journal of College Student Personnel*, 1969, **10**, 193-203. (a)

———. Vocational development of student personnel workers. *Personnel and Guidance Journal*, 1969, **47**, 537-542. (b)

———. Reinterpretation of flat SVIB profiles. *Journal of Vocational Behavior*, 1972, **2**, 201-207.

———, & WALSH, E. P. Exploration of Holland's theory of vocational choice in graduate school environments. *Journal of Vocational Behavior*, 1972, **2**, 223-232.

FROMM, E. *Man for himself*. New York: Rinehart, 1947.

GOUGH, H. G., & HEILBRUN, A. B., JR. Manual for the Adjective Check List. Palo Alto, Calif.: Consulting Psychologists Press, 1965.

GRUNES, W. F. Looking at occupations. *Journal of Abnormal and Social Psychology*, 1957, **54**, 86-92.

GUILFORD, J. P., CHRISTENSEN, P. R., BOND, N. A., JR. & SUTTON, M. A. A factor analysis study of human interests. *Psychological Monographs*, 1954, **68** (4, Whole No. 375).

GUZMAN, M. Study of personality correlates of employees in engineering and accounting occupations. Unpublished masters thesis, University of North Carolina, 1963.

HAASE, R. F. A canonical analysis of the Vocational Preference Inventory and the Strong Vocational Interest Blank. *Journal of Counseling Psychology*, 1971, **18**, 182-183.

HANSEN, J. C., & JOHANSSON, C. B. The application of Holland's vocational model to the Strong Vocational Interest Blank for women. *Journal of Vocational Behavior*, 1972, **2**, 479-493.

HARVEY, D. W. The validity of Holland's Vocational Preference Inventory for adult women. Unpublished doctoral dissertation, University of Connecticut, 1971.

HEIST, P., & YONGE, G. *Manual for the Omnibus Personality Inventory, Form F*. New York: The Psychological Corporation, 1968.

HOGAN, R., HALL, R., & BLANK, E. An extension of the similarity-attraction hypothesis to the study of vocational behavior. Report No. 105. Baltimore: Center for Social Organization of Schools, Johns Hopkins University, 1971.

HOLLAND, J. L. A personality inventory employing occupational titles. *Journal of Applied Psychology*, 1958, **42**, 336-342.

_____. A theory of vocational choice. *Journal of Counseling Psychology*, 1959, 6, 35-45.

_____. Some explorations of a theory of vocational choice: I. One-and two-year longitudinal studies. *Psychological Monographs*, 1962, 76 (26, Whole No. 545).

_____. Explorations of a theory of vocational choice and achievement: II. A four-year prediction study. *Psychological Reports*, 1963, 12, 537-594.

_____. Explorations of a theory of vocational choice: IV. Vocational preferences and their relation to occupational images, daydreams and personality. *Vocational Guidance Quarterly*, published in four parts in Summer, Autumn, and Winter issues. 1963-64.

_____. Explorations of a theory of vocational choice: V. A. one-year prediction study. Moravia, N.Y.: Chronical Guidance Professional Service, 1964.

_____. *Manual for the Vocational Preference Inventory*. Palo Alto, Calif.: Consulting Psychologists Press, 1965.

_____. A psychological classification scheme for vocations and major fields. *Journal of Counseling Psychology*, 1966, 13, 278-288. (a)

_____. *The psychology of vocational choice: A theory of personality types and model environments*. Waltham, Mass.: Blaisdell, 1966. (b)

_____. *ACT guidance profile manual*. Iowa City: The American College Testing Program, 1968. (a)

_____. Explorations of a theory of vocational choice: VI. A longitudinal study using a sample of typical college students. *Journal of Applied Psychology*, 1968, 52, 1-37. (b)

_____. *The self-directed search*. Palo Alto, Calif.: Consulting Psychologists Press, 1970.

_____. *Counselor's guide for the self-directed search*. Palo Alto, Calif.: Consulting Psychologists Press, 1971. (a)

_____. A theory-ridden, computerless, impersonal vocational guidance system. *Journal of Vocational Behavior*, 1971, 1, 167-176. (b)

_____, & LUTZ, S. W. The predictive value of a student's choice of vocation. *Personnel and Guidance Journal*, 1968, 46, 428-436.

HOLLAND, J. L., & NICHOLS, R. C. Explorations of a theory of vocational choice: III. A longitudinal study of change in major field of study. *Personnel and Guidance Journal*, 1964, 43, 235-242.

HOLLAND, J. L., SORENSEN, A. B., CLARK, J. P., NAFZIGER, D. H., & BLUM, Z. D. Applying an occupational classification to a representative sample of work histories. *Journal of Applied Psychology*, 1973, 58, 34-41.

HOLLAND, J. L., VIERNSTEIN, M. C., KUO, H., KARWEIT, N. L., & BLUM, Z. D. A psychological classification of occupations. Journal Supplement Abstract Service, 1972, 2, 84.

HOLLAND, J. L., & WHITNEY, D. R. Changes in the vocational plans of college students: Orderly or random? ACT Research Report No. 25. Iowa City: The American College Testing Program, 1968.

_____, COLE, N. S., & RICHARDS, J. M., JR. An empirical occupational classification derived from a theory of personality and intended for practice and research. ACT Research Report No. 29. Iowa City: The American College Testing Program, 1969.

HOLLANDER, M. A., & PARKER, H. J. Occupational stereotypes and needs: Their relationship to vocational choice. *Vocational Guidance Quarterly*, 1969, **18**, 91-98.

HOPPOCK, R. *Occupational information*. New York: McGraw-Hill, 1968.

HUGHES, H. M., Jr. Vocational choice, level, and consistency: A test of Holland's theory on an employed sample. Unpublished doctoral dissertation, State University of New York at Albany, 1971.

INGRAM, R. T. Holland's typology of personality in the prediction of certain counseling outcomes. Unpublished doctoral dissertation, University of Maryland, 1969.

JARY, P. W. The relationship between job satisfaction of high school principals and their vocational interests as measured by the Holland Vocational Preference Inventory. Unpublished doctoral dissertation, University of Maryland, 1971.

JEANNERET, P. R., & McCORMICK, E. J. The job dimensions of "worker-oriented" job variables and their attribute profiles as based on data from the Position Analysis Questionnaire. Office of Naval Research Contract Nonr-1100(28), Report No. 2. Lafayette, Ind.: Occupational Research Center, Purdue University, 1969.

JOHANSSON, C. B. Cognitive interest styles of students. *Measurement and Evaluation in Guidance*, 1971, **4**, 176-183.

JUNG, C. G. *Psychological types*. New York: Harcourt, Brace, 1933.

KELSO, G. I. The relation of Holland's personality typology to college courses: A test of a theory of vocational choice. Unpublished master's thesis, University of Melbourne, 1969.

KERNEN, P. J. An investigation of personality characteristics of counselees and non-counselees as related to Holland's theory. Unpublished doctoral dissertation, University of North Carolina, 1971.

KIPNIS, D., LANE, G., & BERGER, L. Character structure, vocational interest, and achievement. *Journal of Counseling Psychology*, 1967, **16**, 335-341.

KRISTJANSON, R. W. Personality types and their hypothesized attributes: An application of Holland's vocational choice theory. Unpublished master's thesis, University of North Dakota, 1969.

KRULEE, G. K., O'KEEFE, R., & GOLDBERG, M. Influence of identity processes on student behavior and occupational choice. OE Project No. 5-0809. Northwestern University, 1966.

KUDER, G. F. *Administrator's manual: Kuder Preference Record, Vocational, Form C*. Chicago: Science Research Associates, 1960.

KULBERG, G. E., & OWENS, W. A. Some life history antecedents of engineering interests. *Journal of Educational Psychology*, 1960, **51**, 26-31.

KVALHEIM, G. A replication of parts of Holland's vocational choice theory with a non-select group of high school seniors. Unpublished master's thesis, Wisconsin State University, 1968.

LACEY, D. Holland's vocational models: A study of work groups and need satisfaction. *Journal of Vocational Behavior*, 1971, **1**, 105-122.

LAURENT, H., JR. A study of the developmental backgrounds of men to determine by means of the biographical information blank the relationship between factors in their early backgrounds and their choice of professions. Unpublished doctoral dissertation, Western Reserve University, 1951.

LEE, D. L. Selected interest factors related to academic achievement at the University of North Dakota. Unpublished doctoral dissertation, University of North Dakota, 1970.

_____ , & HEDAHL, B. Holland's personality types applied to the SVIB basic interest scales. *Journal of Vocational Behavior*, 1973, **3**, 61-68.

LINTON, R. *The cultural background of personality*. New York: Century, 1945.

LUCY, W. T. An adult population reflects the stability of Holland's personality types over time. *Journal of College Student Personnel*, 1972, in press.

MARKS, E., & WEBB, S. C. Vocational choice and professional experience as factors in occupational image. *Journal of Applied Psychology*, 1969, **53**, 292-300.

McCormick, E.J., Jeanneret, P.R., & Meacham, R.C. A study of job characteristics and job dimensions as based on the Position Analysis Questionnaire (PAQ). *Journal of Applied Psychology Monograph*, 1972, **56**, 347-368.

McCORMICK, E. J., JEANNERET, P. R., & MECHAM, R. C. The development and background of the Position Analysis Questionnaire. Office of Naval Research Contract Nonr-1100 (28), Report No. 5. Lafayette, Ind.: Occupational Research Center, Purdue University, 1969.

MECHAM, R. C., & McCORMICK, E. J. The rated attribute requirements of job elements in the Position Analysis Questionnaire. Office of Naval Research Contract Nonr-1100 (28), Report No. 1. Lafayette, Ind.: Occupational Research Center, Purdue University, 1969. (a)

_____ . The use of data based on the Position Analysis Questionnaire in developing synthetically-derived attribute requirements of jobs. Office of Naval Research Contract Nonr-1100 (28), Report No. 4. Lafayette, Ind.: Occupational Research Center, Purdue University, 1969. (b)

MEDVENE, A. M. Occupational choice of graduate students in psychology as a function of early parent-child interactions. *Journal of Counseling Psychology*, 1969, **16**, 385-389.

MORROW, J. M., JR. A test of Holland's theory. *Journal of Counseling Psychology*, 1971, **18**, 422-425.

MURRAY, H. A. *Explorations in personality*. New York: Oxford, 1938.

NACHMANN, B. Childhood experience and vocational choice in law, dentistry, and social work. *Journal of Counseling Psychology*, 1960, **7**, 243-250.

NAFZIGER, D. H., HOLLAND, J. L., HELMS, S. T., & McPARTLAND, J. M. Applying an occupational classification to a national representative sample of work histories of young men and women. Research Report No. 132. Baltimore: Center for the Social Organization of Schools, Johns Hopkins University, 1972.

NORMAN, R. D., & BESSEMER, D. W. Job preferences and preference shifts as functions of job information, familiarity, and prestige level. *Journal of Applied Psychology*, 1968, **52**, 280-285.

O'DOWD, D. D., & BEARDSLEE, D. C. College student images of a selected group of professions and occupations. USOE, Cooperative Research Project No. 562 (8142). Middletown, Conn.: Wesleyan University, 1960.

_____ . Development and consistency of student images of occupations. USOE Cooperative Research Project No. 5-0858, Oakland University, 1967.

O'SHEA, A. J., & HARRINGTON, T. F., JR. Strong Vocational Interest Blank and Kuder Occupational Interest Survey differences reexamined in terms of Holland's vocational theory. *Journal of Counseling Psychology*, 1972, **19**, 455-460.

OSIPOW, S. H. Cognitive styles and educational-vocational preferences and selection. *Journal of Counseling Psychology*, 1969, **16**, 534-546.

_____ . The interaction between occupational environments and personality types. In W. Bartlett (Ed.), *Evolving religious careers*. Washington, D.C.: Center for Applied Research in the Apostolate, 1970.

_____ , & ASHBY, J. D. Vocational Preference Inventory high point codes and educational preferences. *Personnel and Guidance Journal*, 1968, **47**, 126-129.

_____ , & WALL, H. W. Personality types and vocational choice: A test of Holland's theory. *Personnel and Guidance Journal*, 1966, **45**, 37-42.

OWENS, W. A. Toward one discipline of scientific psychology. *American Psychologist*, 1968, **23**, 782-785.

PARSONS, F. *Choosing a Vocation*. Boston: Houghton Mifflin, 1909.

PARSONS, G. E. An application of Holland's vocational theory to an empirical study of occupational mobility of men age 45 to 59. Unpublished doctoral dissertation, Ohio State University, 1971.

PATTERSON, T. W., MARRON, J. P., & PATTERSON, N. B. A partial validation of Holland's theory of vocational choice. Paper presented at Rocky Mountain Psychological Association convention, Denver, May 1971.

PETERSON, R. E. *Technical Manual, College Student Questionnaires*. Princeton, N.J.: Educational Testing Service, 1965.

POSTHUMA, A. B., & NAVRAN, L. Relation of congruence in student-faculty interests to achievement in college. *Journal of Counseling Psychology*, 1970, **17**, 352-356.

PRIEBE, J. A. Changes between the 1950 and 1960 occupation and industry classifications. Technical Paper No. 18. Washington, D.C.: U.S. Department of Commerce, Bureau of the Census, 1968.

PRIVATEER, G. J. The effect of a college environment upon an incoming freshman class. Unpublished doctoral dissertation, State University of New York at Buffalo, 1971.

REZLER, A. G. The joint use of the Kuder Preference Record and the Holland Vocational Preference Inventory. *Psychology in the Schools*, 1967, **4**, 82-84.

RICHARDS, J. M., JR. Who studies what major in college. Paper presented at American Psychological convention, Miami, September 1970.

_____ . A study of the "environments" of Japanese universities. Paper presented at Western Psychological Association meeting, San Francisco, April 1971.

_____ , BULKELEY, E. M., & RICHARDS, B. Faculty and curriculum as measures of two-year college environments. Paper presented at American Educational Research convention, New York, 1971.

RICHARDS, J. M., JR., RAND, L. P., & RAND, L. M. Description of junior colleges. *Journal of Educational Psychology*, 1966, **57** 207-214.

RICHARDS, J. M., JR. & SELIGMAN, R. Faculty and curriculum as measures of college environment. Paper presented at American Psychological Association convention, San Francisco, 1969.

———, & JONES, P. K. Faculty and curriculum as measures of college environment. *Journal of Educational Psychology*, 1970, **61**, 324-332.

ROE, A. *The psychology of occupations*. New York: Wiley, 1956.

———, & SIEGELMAN, M. *The origin of interests*. Washington, D.C.: American Personnel and Guidance Association, 1964.

SALOMONE, P. R. Rehabilitation counselor job behavior and vocational personality: Needs and work style. Unpublished doctoral dissertation, University of Iowa, 1968.

———, & MUTHARD, J. E. Canonical correlation of vocational needs and vocational style. *Journal of Vocational Behavior*, 1972, **2**, 163-171.

SCHAEFFER, E. S., & BELL, R. Q. Development of a parental attitude research instrument. *Child Development*, 1958, **29**, 339-361.

SCHULDT, D. L., & STAHMANN, R. F. Interest profiles of clergymen as indicated by the Vocational Preference Inventory. *Educational and Psychological Measurement*, 1971, **31**, 1025-1028.

SCHUTZ, R. A., & BLOCHER, D. H. Self-concepts and stereotypes of vocational preferences. *Vocational Guidance Quarterly*, 1960, **8**, 241-244.

———. Self-satisfaction and level of occupational choice. *Personnel and Guidance Journal*, 1961, **39**, 595-598.

SCOTT, N. A., & SEDLACEK, W. E. Personality differentiation of physical science, engineering and other students. Research Report No. 7-68. College Park, Md.: University of Maryland, Counseling Center, 1968.

SHELDON, W. H. *Atlas of men: A guide for somatotyping the adult male at all ages*. New York: Harper, 1954.

SPRANGER, E. *Types of men*. Translated from the 5th German edition of *Lebensformen* by Paul J. W. Pigors. Halle: Max Niemeyer Verlag, 1928.

STAHMANN, R. F., OSBORN, M. E., & WILLIAMS, C. Vocational interests, job and occupational satisfaction of nuclear medical technologists. Iowa City: College of Medicine, University of Iowa, July 1971.

STOCKIN, B. C. A test of Holland's occupational level formulation. *Personnel and Guidance Journal*, 1964, **54**, 599-602.

STRONG, E. K., JR. *Vocational interests of men and women*. Stanford, Calif: Stanford University Press, 1943.

SUPER, D. E. Vocational development theory: Persons, positions, processes. In J. M. Whiteley, & A. Resnikoff (Eds.), *Perspectives on Vocational Development*. Washington, D.C.: American Personnel and Guidance Association, 1972. Pp. 13-33.

———, & CRITES, J. O. *Appraising vocational fitness* (rev. ed.). New York: Harper and Row, 1962.

U.S. Department of Labor, Manpower Administration. *Dictionary of occupational titles. Vol. II: Occupational classification*. Washington, D.C.: Government Printing Office, 1965.

VIERNSTEIN, M. C. The extension of Holland's occupational classification to all occupations in the Dictionary of Occupational Titles. *Journal of Vocational Behavior*, 1972, **2**, 107-121.

WALL, H. W., OSIPOW, S. H., & ASHBY, J. D. SVIB scores, occupational choices, and Holland's personality types. *Vocational Guidance Quarterly*, 1967, **15**, 201-205.

WALL, R. E. Engineering freshmen responses to the Holland Vocational Preference Inventory and persistence in the University of Maryland College of Engineering. Unpublished doctoral dissertation, University of Maryland, 1969.

————, Choice of major and Vocational Preference Inventory responses. Paper presented at American Personnel and Guidance Association convention, Atlantic City, April 1971.

WALSH, W. B. & BARROW, C. A. Consistent and inconsistent career preferences and personality. *Journal of Vocational Behavior*, 1971, **1**, 271-278.

WALSH, W. B., & LACEY, D. W. Perceived change and Holland's theory. *Journal of Counseling Psychology*, 1969, **16**, 348-352.

————. Further exploration of perceived change and Holland's theory. *Journal of Counseling Psychology*, 1970, **17**, 189-190.

WALSH, W. B., & LEWIS, R. O. Consistent, inconsistent, and undecided career preferences and personality. *Journal of Vocational Behavior*, 1972, **2**, 309-316.

WALSH, W. B., & RUSSELL, J. H. College major choice and personal adjustment. *Personnel and Guidance Journal*, 1969, **47**, 685-688.

WALSH, W. B., VAUDRIN, D. M., & HUMMEL, R. A. The accentuation effect and Holland's theory. *Journal of Vocational Behavior*, 1972, **2**, 77-85.

WERNER, J. E. A study of Holland's theory of vocational choice as it applies to selected working women. Unpublished doctoral dissertation, State University of New York at Buffalo, 1969.

WERNER, W. E. A study of Holland's theory of vocational choice as it applies to vocational high school students. Unpublished doctoral dissertation, State University of New York at Buffalo, 1969.

WERTS, C. E., & WATLEY, D. J. Paternal influence on talent development. Research Report No. 4. Evanston, Ill.: National Merit Scholarship Corporation, 1970.

WHITNEY, D. R. Predicting vocational interests of high ability students. Unpublished paper, 1970.

————, & HOLLAND, J. L. Clustering student personalities to facilitate learning, guidance, and educational administration. Unpublished paper, 1969.

WHITNEY, D. R., & WHITTLESEY, R. R. Tests of two hypotheses about Holland's personality types and counseling outcomes. *Journal of Counseling Psychology*, 1972, **19**, 322-326.

WILLIAMS, C. M. Occupational choice of male graduate students as related to values and personality: A test of Holland's theory. *Journal of Vocational Behavior*, 1972, **2**, 39-46.

WILLIAMS, J. E. Conflict between freshmen male roommates. Research Report No. 10-67. College Park, Md.: University of Maryland, Counseling Center, 1967.

The Vocational Preference Inventory

appendix A

THE VOCATIONAL PREFERENCE INVENTORY

Developed by John L. Holland, Ph.D.

This is an inventory of your feelings and attitudes about many kinds of work. Fill out your answer sheet by following the directions given below:

1. Show on your answer sheet the occupations which *interest* or *appeal* to you by blackening Y for "Yes."

2. Show the occupations which you *dislike* or find *uninteresting* by blackening N for "No."

3. Make *no marks* when you are undecided about an occupation.

---

1. Aviator
2. Private Investigator
3. YMCA Secretary
4. Detective
5. Post Office Clerk
6. Route Salesman
7. Electronic Technician
8. Humorist
9. Photographer
10. Interplanetary Scientist

11. Airplane Mechanic
12. Meteorologist
13. Foreign Missionary
14. Bookkeeper
15. Speculator
16. Poet
17. Deep Sea Diver
18. Newspaper Editor
19. Nursery School Teacher
20. Lawyer

21. Fish and Wildlife Specialist
22. Biologist
23. High School Teacher
24. Quality Control Expert
25. Buyer
26. Symphony Conductor
27. Wrecker (Building)
28. Narcotics Inspector
29. Elementary School Teacher
30. School Principal

31. Power Station Operator
32. Astronomer
33. Juvenile Delinquency Expert
34. Budget Reviewer
35. Stock & Bond Salesman
36. Musician
37. Prize Fighter
38. Diplomat
39. Experimental Laboratory Engineer
40. Crane Operator

41. Master Plumber
42. Aeronautical Design Engineer
43. Speech Therapist
44. Traffic Manager
45. Manufacturer's Representative
46. Author
47. Fireman
48. Army General
49. Interior Decorator
50. Novelist

51. Power Shovel Operator
52. Anthropologist
53. Marriage Counselor
54. Statistician
55. Television Producer
56. Commercial Artist
57. Wild Animal Trainer
58. U.N. Official
59. Sculptor
60. Automobile Mechanic

61. Surveyor
62. Zoologist
63. Physical Education Teacher
64. Court Stenographer
65. Hotel Manager
66. Free-Lance Writer
67. Stunt Man (Motion Picture)
68. Criminal Lawyer
69. Professional Athlete
70. Carpenter

71. Construction Inspector
72. Chemist
73. Playground Director
74. Bank Teller
75. Business Executive
76. Musical Arranger
77. Jockey
78. Ventriloquist
79. Army Officer
80. Banker

81. Radio Operator
82. Independent Research Scientist
83. Clinical Psychologist
84. Tax Expert
85. Restaurant Worker
86. Art Dealer
87. Motorcycle Driver
88. Police Judge
89. Referee (Sporting Events)
90. Truck Gardener

91. Filling Station Attendant
92. Writer of Scientific or Technical Articles
93. Social Science Teacher
94. Inventory Controller
95. Master of Ceremonies
96. Dramatic Coach
97. Blaster (Dynamiter)
98. Mind Reader
99. English Teacher
100. Sales Manager

101. Tree Surgeon
102. Editor of a Scientific Journal
103. Director of Welfare Agency
104. IBM Equipment Operator
105. Traveling Salesman
106. Concert Singer
107. F.B.I. Agent
108. Prosecuting Attorney
109. Factory Foreman
110. College Professor

111. Tool Designer
112. Geologist
113. Asst. City School Superintendent
114. Financial Analyst
115. Real Estate Salesman
116. Composer
117. Mountain Climber
118. Congressional Investigator
119. Portrait Artist
120. Machinist

121. Locomotive Engineer
122. Botanist
123. Personal Counselor
124. Cost Estimator
125. Industrial Relations Consultant
126. Stage Director
127. Explorer
128. Supreme Court Judge
129. Draftsman
130. Judge

131. Photoengraver
132. Scientific Research Worker
133. Psychiatric Case Worker
134. Pay Roll Clerk
135. Sports Promoter
136. Playwright
137. Test Pilot
138. Criminologist
139. Children's Clothing Designer
140. Truck Driver

141. Electrician
142. Physicist
143. Vocational Counselor
144. Bank Examiner
145. Political Campaign Manager
146. Cartoonist
147. Racing Car Driver
148. Book Censor
149. Social Worker
150. Locksmith

151. Funeral Director
152. Counter-Intelligence Man
153. Architect
154. Shipping & Receiving Clerk
155. Criminal Psychologist
156. Insurance Clerk
157. Barber
158. Bill Collector
159. Ward Attendant
160. Masseur

The Occupational Classification

appendix B

THE OCCUPATIONS FINDER

The 456 occupations in this classification include all of the most common occupations in the United States. They are arranged in a system that uses the code letters (R, I, A, S, E, C).

Realistic occupations (R) include skilled trades, technical and some service occupations.

Investigative occupations (I) include scientific and some technical occupations.

Artistic occupations (A) include artistic, musical, and literary occupations.

Social occupations (S) include educational and social welfare occupations.

Enterprising occupations (E) include managerial and sales occupations.

Conventional occupations (C) include office and clerical occupations.

The three-letter codes provide descriptions of occupations. For example, the code of ESC for salesmen means that salesmen resemble people in Enterprising occupations most of all, that they resemble people in Social occupations somewhat less, and people in Conventional occupations still less. In this way, the codes provide a brief summary of what an occupation is like by showing its degrees of resemblance to three occupational groups.

There are a few combinations of the code letters which do not occur at all, or which occur very infrequently. In such cases a person may use a two-letter rather than a three-letter code and study the nature of all the occupations with that code.

The single digit indicates the level of general educational development an occupation demands. Levels 5 and 6 mean college training is necessary. Levels 3 and 4 mean high school and some college, technical, or business training is needed. Levels 1 and 2 mean that an occupation requires only elementary school training or no special training at all. In general, these levels are only estimates and should not be regarded as precise requirements.

The six-digit number is from the *Dictionary of Occupational Titles* (DOT), which can be found in most libraries and employment and counseling offices. The DOT contains descriptions of occupations and estimates of interests and aptitudes associated with each occupation.

Using the six-digit code and the DOT, it is possible to extend one's understanding of any occupation listed and this process is a very important part of *The Self-Directed Search.* A further step might involve locating a place which employs workers in a particular occupation and observing the work, talking to the employees about their jobs and to the supervisors or employment officers about job qualifications, training, and opportunities.

Unless a person is unusually well-informed about the world of work, there will be many occupations in *The Occupations Finder* that he has never heard of, some that sound humorous, and some that he is "sure" he would never enjoy, even though he has little knowledge of what the occupation is like. One should not reject an occupation until he fully understands it.

Additional useful information about occupations can be obtained from the *Occupational Outlook Handbook,* U.S. Department of Labor, Bureau of Labor Statistics, which is published every two years. (See your counselor or library, or write Superintendent of Documents, U.S. Government Printing Office, Washington, D.C., 20402, and enclose a check for $6.25.) This handbook provides a wide range of information about occupations, income, training, and employment trends.

REALISTIC OCCUPATIONS

	ED		ED
CODE: RIA		**(RIS con't.)**	
Architectural Draftsman (017.281)	4	Miller/Foreman (521.130)	4
Dental Technician (712.381)	4	Jeweler (700.281)	4
		Power Plant Operator (950.782)	4
CODE: RIS		Powerhouse Repairman (631.281)	4
Forester (040.081)	5	Skilled Tradesman*	4
Industrial Arts Teacher (091.228)	5	Tool and Die Maker (601.280)	4
Radio Operator (003.187)	5	Glazier (638.281)	4
Electrician (820.281)	4	Loom Fixer (683.280)	4

Not elsewhere classified.

REALISTIC OCCUPATIONS (Continued)

CODE: RIS (con't.)	ED
Baker (526.781)	3
Cook (315.381)	3
Filling Station Attendant (915.867)	3
Heat Treater (504.782)	3
Optician (713.381)	3
Welder (812.884)	3
Wire Drawer (614.782)	3
Offset Press Operator (651.885)	2

CODE: RIE	ED
Automotive Engineer (007.081)	6
Mechanical Engineer (007.081)	6
Engineer, Mining (010.081)	5
Civil Engineer (005.081)	5
Industrial Engineer Technician (012.288)	5
Mechanical Engineer Technician 007.181)	5
Aircraft Mechanic (621.281)	4
Air Traffic Controller (193.168)	4
Automobile Mechanic (620.281)	4
Watch Repairman (715.281)	4
Boilermaker (805.281)	4
Draftsman (017.281)	4
Electroplater (500.380)	4
Garage Foreman (620.131)	4
Farmer (Rancher) (421.181)	4
Lineman (tel. & tel.) (822.381)	4
Loom Changer (683.380)	4
Machine Repairman (600.280)	4
Machinist (600.280)	4
Maintenance Man (899.281)	4
Milwright (638.281)	4
Mechanic, Radio (823.281)	4
Mechanic* (600.280)	4
Plumber (862.381)	4
Sheet Metal Man (804.281)	4
Automobile Body Repairman (807.381)	3
Compressor House Operator (953.782)	3
Engraver, Machine (704.884)	3
Forging Press Operator (611.782)	3
Heavy Equipment Operator (859.883)	3
Roofer (866.381)	3
Upholsterer (806.887)	3
Logger (940.884)	2
Machine Operator*	2
Tool Crib Attendant (223.387)	2

CODE: RIC	ED
Load Checker (952.387)	4
Stone Cutter (771.281)	4
Turret Lathe Operator (604.380)	4
Elevator Mechanic (829.281)	4
Locksmith (709.281)	4
Nuclear Reactor Technician (015.380)	4
Nurseryman (406.168)	4
Tree Surgeon (409.181)	4
Piano Tuner (730.381)	4
Switchman (tel. & tel.) (822.281)	4

CODE: RIC (con't.)	ED
Assembler (827.884)	3
Drill Press Operator (606.782)	3
Dry Cleaner (362.782)	3
Grinder* (603.782)	3
Inspector (504.387)	3
Roller (613.782)	3
Printer (651.782)	3
Shipping/Receiving Clerk (222.387)	3
Structural Steel Worker (801.781)	3
Tire Builder (750.884)	3
Shoe Repairman (365.381)	3
Teamster (919.883)	2
Grounds Keeper (407.884)	2

CODE: RAI	ED
Compositor (Typesetter) (973.381)	4
Bookbinder (977.884)	3

CODE: RSE	ED
Blacksmith (610.381)	4
Fireman, Locomotive (910.383)	4
Gas Main-Fitter (862.381)	4
Molder (Foundry) (518.381)	4
Pipeman (862.381)	4
Railroad Conductor (198.168)	4
Barber (330.371)	3
Butcher (316.884)	3
Policeman (Patrolman) (375.268)	3
Detective (376.868)	3
Coal Equipment Operator (922.883)	3
Fireman (Fire Fighter) (373.884)	3
Motorman (Streetcar) (913.363)	3
Taxicab Driver (913.463)	3
Chauffeur (913.883)	3
Waitress (Waiter) (311.878)	3
Fountain Man (319.878)	2
Laborer, Guard, Janitor, Watchman, Warehouseman*	2
Parking Lot Attendant (915.878)	2

CODE: RSC	ED
Bill Collector (240.368)	3
Elevator Operator (388.868)	2
Stockman (929.887)	2
Kitchen Helper (318.887)	1

CODE: RSI	ED
Vocational Agriculture Teacher (091.228)	5
Gas Appliance Serviceman (637.281)	4
Weaver (683.782)	3
Knitter (685.885)	2

CODE: REC	ED
Laundress (302.887)	2
Maid (323.887)	2

CODE: REI	ED
Air Conditioning Engineer Mechanic (637.281)	4

*Not elsewhere classified.

REALISTIC OCCUPATIONS (Continued)

CODE: REI (con't.)	ED	CODE: RCS	ED
Foreman (530.132)	4	Installer Repairman (822.281)	4
Ship Pilot (197.133)	4	Tailor (785.261)	4
Trackman (869.887)	2	Seamstress (785.381)	3
		Tile Setter (861.781)	3
CODE: RES	**ED**	Blaster (859.281)	3
Fish and Game Warden (379.168)	5	Bricklayer (861.381)	3
Railroad Engineer (910.383)	4	Bus Driver (913.463)	3
Cattle Rancher (413.181)	4	Cement Mason (844.884)	3
Crater and Packer (920.884)	3	Dressmaker (785.361)	3
Railroad Brakeman (910.884)	3	Furnaceman (558.782)	3
Stock Clerk (223.387)	3	Mail Carrier (233.388)	3
Fisherman (431.884)	2	Meter Reader (239.588)	3
		Miner (850.781)	3
CODE: RCI	**ED**	Sailor (Seaman) (911.887)	3
Surveyor (081.188)	5	Plasterer (842.781)	3
Instrument Mechanic (710.281)	4	Industrial Truck Operator (922.883)	2
Motion Picture Projectionist		Spinner (682.885)	2
(960.382)	4	**CODE: RCE**	**ED**
Typewriter Repairman (633.281)	4	Craneman (921.883)	3
Carpenter (860.381)	4	Grader (589.687)	3
Painter (House, Building, Equipment)		Truck Driver (905.883)	3
(840.781)	3	Tractor Operator (929.883)	3
Rodman (018.587)	3	Fork Lift Operator (922.883)	2

INVESTIGATIVE OCCUPATIONS

CODE: IAS	ED	CODE: IES (con't.)	ED
Economist (050.088)	6	Pharmacist (074.181)	5
Internist (Physician) (070.108)	6	Research Analyst (011.281)	4
CODE: IAR	**ED**	**CODE: IEC**	**ED**
Anthropologist (055.088)	6	Actuary (020.188)	5
Astronomer (021.088)	6	**CODE: ICR**	**ED**
Pathologist (070.108)	6	Quality Control Technician	
Physicist (023.081)	6	(019.281)	5
Chemist (022.081)	6	Computer Operator (213.382)	4
CODE: ISC	**ED**	Equipment Repairman (620.281)	4
Production Planner (012.188)	5	Research Assistant (199.384)	4
Medical-Laboratory Assistant		**CODE: IRA**	**ED**
(078.381)	4	Geologist (024.081)	6
Repairman, TV (720.281)	4	Mathematician, Statistician (020.088)	6
CODE: ISR	**ED**	Surgeon (070.108)	6
Biologist (041.081)	6	Meterologist (025.088)	5
Osteopath (071.108)	6	Weather Observer (025.288)	5
Chiropractor (079.108)	5	**CODE: IRS**	**ED**
Mathematics Teacher (091.228)	5	Agronomist (040.081)	6
Natural Science Teacher (091.228)	5	Animal Scientist (040.081)	6
Optometrist (079.108)	5	Botanist (041.081)	6
CODE: ISA	**ED**	Horticulturist (040.081)	6
Physician* (070.108)	6	Natural Scientist* (023.081)	6
Psychiatrist (070.108)	6	Oceanographer (024.081)	6
Psychologist (045.088)	6	Zoologist (041.081)	6
Medical Technologist (078.381)	5	Biochemist (041.081)	6
CODE: IES	**ED**	Engineer Aide (007.181)	5
Bacteriologist (041.081)	6	Veterinarian (073.108)	5
Physiologist (041.081)	6	Geographer (029.088)	5
		X-Ray Technician (078.368)	4

*Not elsewhere classified.

INVESTIGATIVE OCCUPATIONS (Continued)

CODE: IRE	ED	CODE: IRE (con't.)	ED
Administrator, Engineer (002.081)	6	Electronic Technician (729.381)	4
Aeronautical Engineer (002.081)	6	Metallurgist, Assistant (011.281)	4
Chemical Engineer (008.081)	6		
Dentist (072.108)	6	**CODE: IRC**	**ED**
Electrical Engineer (003.081)	6	Airplane Navigator (196.188)	5
Metallurgical Engineer (011.081)	6	Computer Programmer (020.188)	5
Test Engineer, Aircraft (002.081)	6	Tool Designer (007.081)	5
Engineer* (007.081)	6	Model Maker (149.281)	5
Chemical Laboratory Technician		Airplane Pilot (196.283)	5
(022.281)	5	Engineering Technician* (007.181)	5
Radio or Television Engineer		Instrument Repairman (710.281)	4
(003.081)	5	Laboratory Technician (029.381)	4
Aerospace Engineering Technician	4	Tester, Electronic Systems (729.381)	4
		Tool Maker (601.280)	4

ARTISTIC OCCUPATIONS

CODE: ASE	ED	CODE: AIS	ED
Drama Coach (150.028)	5	Writer (130.088)	6
English Teacher (091.228)	5	Editor (132.038)	6
Journalist-Reporter (132.268)	5	Radio Program Writer (130.088)	6
Drama Teacher (150.028)	5	Dramatist (131.088)	6
Dancing Teacher (151.028)	5	Actor-Actress (150.048)	5
Foreign Language Interpreter		Designer (142.081)	5
(137.268)	5	Interior Decorator (142.051)	5
		Critic (Reviewer) (132.088)	5
CODE: ASI	**ED**	Fashion Illustrator (141.081)	5
Philosopher (090.228)	6	Furniture Designer (142.081)	5
Art Teacher (149.028)	5	Jewelry Designer (142.081)	5
Literature Teacher (091.228)	5	Furrier (142.081)	4
Music Teacher (152.028)	5	Women's Garment Designer	
Musician (152.048)	5	(142.081)	4
Orchestra Leader (152.048)	5	**CODE: AIE**	**ED**
CODE: AES	**ED**	Decorator (298.381)	4
Advertising Man (164.068)	5	**CODE: AIR**	**ED**
Advertising Manager (164.118)	5	Architect (001.081)	6
Entertainer (Dancer, Singer)		Artist (144.081)	5
(159.048)	5	Photographer (143.062)	4
Public Relations Man (165.068)	5	Photolithographer (972.382)	4
Fashion Model (297.868)	3	Photograph Retoucher (970.281)	3

SOCIAL OCCUPATIONS

CODE: SEC	ED	CODE: SER	ED
Director Social Service (195.118)	6	Claim Adjuster (241.168)	5
Compensation Advisor (169.118)	5	Production Expediter (221.168)	5
Dorm Director (045.108)	5	Health & Welfare Coordinator	
Employment Representative (166.268)	5	(166.168)	4
Funeral Director (187.168)	5		
Interviewer (166.268)	5	**CODE: SEI**	**ED**
Job Analyst (166.088)	5	Educational Administrator (090.118)	6
Chamber of Commerce Executive		Training Director (166.118)	6
(187.118)	5	Environmental Health Engineer	
Employee Benefits Approver (166.168)	4	(079.118)	5
Food Service Manager (319.138)	4	Historian (052.088)	5
Bartender (312.878)	3	History Teacher (091.228)	5
Hostess (Hotel, Tea Room, Etc.)		Home Service Representative	
(310.868)	3	(278.258)	5

*Not elsewhere classified.

SOCIAL OCCUPATIONS (Continued)

CODE: SEA	ED
Community Recreation Administrator	6
Counselor* (045.108)	5
Foreign Service Officer (188.118)	5

CODE: SCE	ED
Recreation Director (187.118)	6
Business Agent, Labor Union (187.118)	5
Executive Housekeeper (187.168)	5
Public Health Service Officer (187.118)	5
Theatre Manager (187.168)	5
Caterer (187.168)	4
Liquor Store Manager (187.168)	4
Restaurant Proprietor (187.168)	4
Order Service Correspondent (204.288)	4
Ticket Agent (919.368)	4
Baggageman (Motor Transportation) (358.878)	3

CODE: SRI	ED
Extension Agent (096.128)	5

CODE: SRE	ED
Athletic Coach (099.228)	5
Physical Education Teacher (153.228)	5
Building Superintendent (187.168)	5
Housekeeper (321.138)	4
Occupational Therapist (079.128)	4
Governess (099.228)	4
Athlete (153.348)	3
Houseparent (359.878)	3

CODE: SRC	ED
Ward Attendant (359.878)	3

CODE: SIA	ED
College Professor (090.228)	6
Political Scientist (051.088)	6
Social Scientist*	6
Sociologist (054.088)	6
Professional Nurse (075.378)	5
Social Worker (195.108)	5
Group Worker (195.108)	5
Rehabilitation Counselor (045.108)	5

CODE: SIE	ED
Building Inspector (168.168)	5
Personnel Director (166.118)	5
Dietitian (077.168)	4
Inspector, Public Admin. (168.287)	4
Customs Inspector (168.168)	4

CODE: SIC	ED
School Superintendent (091.118)	6
Food and Drug Inspector (168.287)	5
Politician	5
Social Science Teacher (091.228)	5
YMCA Physical Director (195.168)	5
YMCA Secretary (195.168)	5
Parole Officer (195.108)	5

CODE: SIR	ED
Podiatrist (Foot Doctor) (079.108)	5
Physical Therapist (079.378)	4
Therapist*	

CODE: SAE	ED
Home Economist (096.128)	5
Housewife	
Home Economics Teacher (091.228)	5
Foreign Language Teacher (091.228)	5
Speech Teacher (091.228)	5
Teacher*	5

CODE: SAC	ED
Cosmetologist (332.271)	4
Electrologist (339.371)	4
Hair Stylist (332.271)	4
Manicurist (331.878)	2

CODE: SAI	ED
Clergyman (120.108)	6
Elementary Teacher (092.228)	5
Librarian (100.168)	5
Special Education Teacher (094.228)	5
Speech and Hearing Clinician (079.108)	5
Dental Assistant (079.378)	4
Dental Hygienist (078.368)	4
Licensed Practical Nurse (079.378)	4

ENTERPRISING OCCUPATIONS

CODE: ECI	ED
Market Analyst (050.088)	6
Banker (186.118)	5

CODE: ECS	ED
Grain Buyer (162.168)	5
Insurance Underwriter (169.188)	5
Real Estate Appraiser (191.287)	5
Buyer (Purchasing Agent) (162.158)	4
Real Estate Salesman (250.358)	4
Supervisor, Ticket Sales (912.138)	4
Florist (Dealer) (162.158)	4
Art Goods Dealer (162.158)	4
Furniture Dealer (162.158)	4

CODE: ERI	ED
Industrial Engineer (012.188)	6
Farm Manager (409.168)	4
Contractor (182.168)	4

CODE: ERS	ED
Warehouse Manager (184.168)	5

CODE: ERC	ED
Postmaster (188.168)	4

CODE: EIS	ED
Salesman, Technical Products (284.258)	5

*Not elsewhere classified.

ENTERPRISING OCCUPATIONS (Continued)

CODE: EAS	ED	CODE: ESR	ED
Lawyer, Judge, Attorney (110.118)	6	Sporting Goods Salesman (286.358)	4
		Route Salesman (292.358)	3

CODE: EAR	ED
Radio/TV Announcer (159.148)	5

CODE: ESI	ED
Director of Admin. Services (195.118)	6

CODE: ESC	ED
Administrative Assistant (169.168)	5
Branch Manager (186.118)	5
Director, Industrial Relations (166.118)	5
Employment Interviewer (166.268)	5
Government Official	5
Insurance Manager (186.118)	5
Manager/Administrator*	
Operations Manager (184.118)	5
Manager, Restaurant/Bar (187.168)	5
Personnel Assistant (166.118)	5
Personnel Manager (166.168)	5
Personnel Recruiter (166.268)	5
Production Manager (183.118)	5
Salary & Wage Administrator (169.118)	5
Sales Manager (163.118)	5
Traffic Manager (184.168)	5
Business Manager (191.118)	5
Labor Arbitrator (169.118)	5
Office Manager (169.168)	5
Customer Services Manager (912.138)	4
Apartment House Manager (186.168)	4
Insurance Investigator (191.268)	4
Demonstrator (297.458)	3
Dispatcher, Motor Vehicle (919.168)	3
Peddler (Huckster) (291.858)	3
Sales Clerk (290.478)	3
Salesman*	3

CODE: ESI (cont.)	ED
Systems Analyst, Business EDP (012.168)	5
Director, Compensation & Benefits (166.168)	4
Life Insurance Salesman (250.258)	4
Manpower Adviser (166.168)	4
Encyclopedia Salesman	4
Automobile Dealer (185.168)	4
Gas Station Manager (185.168)	4
Gift Shop Manager (185.168)	4
Grocer (185.168)	4
Importer-Exporter (Wholesaler) (185.168)	4
Retail Merchant (185.168)	4
Shoe Store Manager (185.168)	4

CODE: ESA	ED
Security Salesman (251.258)	6
Director, Recreation (352.878)	4
Guide, Travel (353.168)	4
Salesperson, Photographic Equipment and Supplies (285.358)	4
Salesperson, Musical Instruments and Accessories (287.358)	3
Airline Stewardess (352.878)	3

CONVENTIONAL OCCUPATIONS

CODE: CRI	ED
Timekeeper (215.488)	4
Biller (219.388)	3
Key Punch Operator (213.582)	3
Tabulating Machine Operator (213.782)	3
Duplicating Machine Operator (207.782)	3

CODE: CRS	ED
File Clerk (206.388)	3
Teller (211.468)	3

CODE: CRE	ED
Sewing Machine Operator (787.782)	3
Instrument Assembler	

CODE: CIS	ED
Certified Public Accountant (160.188)	5
Time Study Analyst (012.188)	5
Auto Writing Machine Operator (215.388)	4
Bookkeeping Machine Operator (215.388)	4
Estimator (book publishing) (219.388)	4
Foreign Trade Clerk (219.488)	4

CODE: CIS (con't.)	ED
Calculating Machine Operator (216.488)	3
Accounting/Statistical Clerk (219.488)	3
High-Speed Printer Operator (213.382)	3

CODE: CIE	ED
Office Worker*	4
Payroll Clerk (215.488)	4
Proofreader (209.688)	3
Typist (203.588)	3

CODE: CIR	ED
Accounting Machine Operator (215.388)	4
Office Machine Operator (216.488)	3
Telegraph Operator (203.588)	3

CODE: CSE	ED
Business (Commercial) Teacher (091.228)	5
Personnel Clerk (205.368)	4
Sales Correspondent (204.388)	4
Travel Bureau Clerk (237.368)	4
Receptionist (237.368)	3
Telephone Operator (235.862)	3

*Not elsewhere classified.

CONVENTIONAL OCCUPATIONS (Continued)

CODE: CSR	ED	CODE: CER	ED
Reservations Agent (912.368)	4	Data Processing Worker	4
Traffic Checker (919.368)	3	Mail Clerk (232.268)	4

CODE: CSI	ED	CODE: CEI	ED
Bookkeeper (210.388)	4	Finance Expert (020.188)	5
Cashier (211.368)	4	Personnel Secretary (201.368)	4

CODE: CSA	ED	CODE: CES	ED
Secretary* (201.368)	4	Accountant (160.188)	5
Medical Secretary (201.368)	4	Credit Manager (168.168)	5
Library Assistant (249.368)	4	Clerk* (209.388)	3
Religious Affairs Clerk (249.368)	3	Clerk-Stenographer (202.388)	3

Not elsewhere classified.

The Self-directed Search

appendix C

■ OCCUPATIONAL DAYDREAMS

1. List below the occupations you have considered in thinking about your future. List the careers you have daydreamed about as well as those you have discussed with others. Try to give a history of your tentative choices and daydreams. Put your most recent job choice on Line 1 and work backwards to the earlier jobs you have considered.

Occupation   Code

1. _____   ☐ ☐ ☐

2. _____   ☐ ☐ ☐

3. _____   ☐ ☐ ☐

4. _____   ☐ ☐ ☐

5. _____   ☐ ☐ ☐

6. _____   ☐ ☐ ☐

7. _____   ☐ ☐ ☐

8. _____   ☐ ☐ ☐

2. Now use *The Occupations Finder*. Locate the three-letter code for each of the occupations you just wrote down. This search for occupational codes will help you learn about the many occupations in the world. This task usually takes from 5 to 15 minutes.

If you can't find the exact occupation in *The Occupations Finder*, use the occupation that seems most like your occupational choice.

◼ ◼ ACTIVITIES

Blacken under "L" for those activities you like to do. Blacken under "D" for those things you are indifferent to, have never done, or do not like.

Realistic

	L	D
Fix electrical things	☐	☐
Repair cars	☐	☐
Fix mechanical things	☐	☐
Build things with wood	☐	☐
Drive a truck or tractor	☐	☐
Use metalworking or machine tools	☐	☐
Work on a hot rod or motorcycle	☐	☐
Take Shop course	☐	☐
Take Mechanical drawing course	☐	☐
Take Woodworking course	☐	☐
Take Auto mechanics course	☐	☐

Total No. of L's ☐

Investigative

	L	D
Read scientific books or magazines	☐	☐
Work in a laboratory	☐	☐
Work on a scientific project	☐	☐
Build rocket models	☐	☐
Work with a chemistry set	☐	☐
Read about special subjects on my own	☐	☐
Solve math or chess puzzles	☐	☐
Take Physics course	☐	☐
Take Chemistry course	☐	☐
Take Geometry course	☐	☐
Take Biology course	☐	☐

Total No. of L's ☐

Artistic

	L	D
Sketch, draw, or paint	☐	☐
Attend plays	☐	☐
Design furniture or buildings	☐	☐
Play in a band, group, or orchestra	☐	☐
Practice a musical instrument	☐	☐
Go to recitals, concerts, or musicals	☐	☐
Read popular fiction	☐	☐
Create portraits or photographs	☐	☐
Read plays	☐	☐
Read or write poetry	☐	☐
Take Art course	☐	☐

Total No. of L's ☐

Social

	L	D
Write letters to friends	☐	☐
Attend religious services	☐	☐
Belong to social clubs	☐	☐
Help others with their personal problems	☐	☐
Take care of children	☐	☐
Go to parties	☐	☐
Dance	☐	☐
Read psychology books	☐	☐
Attend meetings and conferences	☐	☐
Go to sports events	☐	☐
Make new friends	☐	☐

Total No. of L's ☐

Enterprising

	L	D
Influence others	☐	☐
Sell something	☐	☐
Discuss politics	☐	☐
Operate my own service or business	☐	☐
Attend conferences	☐	☐
Give talks	☐	☐
Serve as an officer of any group	☐	☐
Supervise the work of others	☐	☐
Meet important people	☐	☐
Lead a group in accomplishing some goal	☐	☐
Participate in political campaign	☐	☐

Total No. of L's ☐

Conventional

	L	D
Keep your desk and room neat	☐	☐
Type papers or letters for yourself or for others	☐	☐
Add, subtract, multiply, and divide numbers in business, or bookkeeping	☐	☐
Operate business machines of any kind	☐	☐
Keep detailed records of expenses	☐	☐
Take Typewriting course	☐	☐
Take Business course	☐	☐
Take Bookkeeping course	☐	☐
Take Commercial math course	☐	☐
File letters, reports, records, etc.	☐	☐
Write business letters	☐	☐

Total No. of L's ☐

■ ■ ■ COMPETENCIES

Blacken under Y for "Yes" for those activities you can do well or competently. Blacken under N for "No" for those activities you have never performed or perform poorly.

Realistic   Y   N

I have used wood shop power tools such as power saw   □   □
   or lathe
I know how to use a voltmeter   □   □
I can adjust a carburetor   □   □
I have operated metal shop power tools such as a drill   □   □
   press or grinder
I can refinish varnished or stained furniture or woodwork   □   □
I can read blueprints   □   □
I can make simple electrical repairs   □   □
I can repair furniture   □   □
I can make mechanical drawings   □   □
I can make simple repairs on a TV set   □   □
I can make simple plumbing repairs   □   □

                       Total No. of Y's ☐

Investigative

I understand how a vacuum tube works   □   □
I can name three foods that are high in protein content   □   □
I understand the "half-life" of a radioactive element   □   □
I can use logarithmic tables   □   □
I can use a slide rule to multiply or divide   □   □
I can use a microscope   □   □
I can identify three constellations of the stars   □   □
I can describe the function of the white blood cells   □   □
I can interpret simple chemical formulae   □   □
I understand why man-made satellites do not fall to the earth   □   □
I have participated in a scientific fair or contest   □   □

                       Total No. of Y's ☐

Artistic

I can play a musical instrument   □   □
I can participate in two- or four-part choral singing   □   □
I can perform as a musical soloist   □   □
I can act in a play   □   □
I can do interpretive reading   □   □
I can do modern interpretive or ballet dancing   □   □
I can sketch people so that they can be recognized   □   □
I can do a painting or sculpture   □   □
I can make pottery   □   □
I can design clothing, posters, or furniture   □   □
I write stories or poetry well   □   □

                       Total No. of Y's ☐

Social   Y N

I am good at explaining things to others
I have participated in charity or benefit drives
I cooperate and work well with others
I am competent at entertaining people older than I
I can be a good host (hostess)
I can teach children easily
I can plan entertainment for a party
I am good at helping people who are upset or troubled
I have worked as a volunteer aide in a hospital, clinic,
    or home
I can plan school or church social affairs
I am a good judge of personality

Total No. of Y's ☐

Enterprising

I have been elected to an office in high school or college
I can supervise the work of others
I have unusual energy and enthusiasm
I am good at getting people to do things my way
I am a good salesman
I have acted as spokesman for some group in presenting
    suggestions or complaints to a person in authority
I won an award for work as a salesman or leader
I have organized a club, group, or gang
I have started my own business or service
I know how to be a successful leader
I am a good debater

Total No. of Y's ☐

Conventional

I can type 40 words a minute
I can operate a duplicating or adding machine
I can take shorthand
I can file correspondence and other papers
I have held an office job
I can use a bookkeeping machine
I can do a lot of paper work in a short time
I can use a calculating machine
I can use simple data processing equipment such as
    a keypuch
I can post credits and debits
I can keep accurate records of payments or sales

Total No. of Y's ☐

■ ▓ ▓ ▓ OCCUPATIONS

This is an inventory of your feelings and attitudes about many kinds of work.
Show the occupations that *interest* or *appeal* to you by blackening under
Y for "Yes." Show the occupations that you *dislike* or find *uninteresting* by
blackening under N for "No."

	Y	N		Y	N
Airplane Mechanic	☐	☐	Foreign Missionary	☐	☐
Fish and Wildlife Specialist	☐	☐	High School Teacher	☐	☐
Power Station Operator	☐	☐	Juvenile Delinquency Expert	☐	☐
Master Plumber	☐	☐	Speech Therapist	☐	☐
Power Shovel Operator	☐	☐	Marriage Counselor	☐	☐
Surveyor	☐	☐	Physical Education Teacher	☐	☐
Construction Inspector	☐	☐	Playground Director	☐	☐
Radio Operator	☐	☐	Clinical Psychologist	☐	☐
Filling Station Attendant	☐	☐	Social Science Teacher	☐	☐
Tree Surgeon	☐	☐	Director of Welfare Agency	☐	☐
Tool Designer	☐	☐	Asst. City School Supt.	☐	☐
Locomotive Engineer	☐	☐	Personal Counselor	☐	☐
Photoengraver	☐	☐	Psychiatric Case Worker	☐	☐
Electrician	☐	☐	Vocational Counselor	☐	☐
Total Realistic Y's ☐			Total Social Y's ☐		
Meteorologist	☐	☐	Speculator	☐	☐
Biologist	☐	☐	Buyer	☐	☐
Astronomer	☐	☐	Stock & Bond Salesman	☐	☐
Aeronautical Design Engineer	☐	☐	Manufacturer's Representative	☐	☐
Anthropologist	☐	☐	Television Producer	☐	☐
Zoologist	☐	☐	Hotel Manager	☐	☐
Chemist	☐	☐	Business Executive	☐	☐
Independent Research Scientist	☐	☐	Restaurant Worker	☐	☐
Writer of Scientific Articles	☐	☐	Master of Ceremonies	☐	☐
Editor of a Scientific Journal	☐	☐	Traveling Salesman	☐	☐
Geologist	☐	☐	Real Estate Salesman	☐	☐
Botanist	☐	☐	Industrial Relations Consultant	☐	☐
Scientific Research Worker	☐	☐	Sports Promoter	☐	☐
Physicist	☐	☐	Political Campaign Manager	☐	☐
Total Investigative Y's ☐			Total Enterprising Y's ☐		
Poet	☐	☐	Bookkeeper	☐	☐
Symphony Conductor	☐	☐	Quality Control Expert	☐	☐
Musician	☐	☐	Budget Reviewer	☐	☐
Author	☐	☐	Traffic Manager	☐	☐
Commercial Artist	☐	☐	Statistician	☐	☐
Free-Lance Writer	☐	☐	Court Stenographer	☐	☐
Musical Arranger	☐	☐	Bank Teller	☐	☐
Art Dealer	☐	☐	Tax Expert	☐	☐
Dramatic Coach	☐	☐	Inventory Controller	☐	☐
Concert Singer	☐	☐	IBM Equipment Operator	☐	☐
Composer	☐	☐	Financial Analyst	☐	☐
Stage Director	☐	☐	Cost Estimator	☐	☐
Playwright	☐	☐	Payroll Clerk	☐	☐
Cartoonist	☐	☐	Bank Examiner	☐	☐
Total Artistic Y's ☐			Total Conventional Y's ☐		

■ ■ ■ ■ ■ **SELF-ESTIMATES**

1. Rate yourself on each of the following traits as *you really think you are when compared with other persons your own age*. Give the most accurate estimate of *how you see yourself*. Circle the appropriate number and *avoid rating yourself the same in each ability*.

	Mechanical Ability	Scientific Ability	Artistic Ability	Teaching Ability	Sales Ability	Clerical Ability	
High	7	7	7	7	7	7	LETTERS WITH HIGHEST RATINGS
	6	6	6	6	6	6	
	5	5	5	5	5	5	□ 1st
Average	4	4	4	4	4	4	
	3	3	3	3	3	3	□ 2nd
	2	2	2	2	2	2	
Low	1	1	1	1	1	1	□ 3rd
	R	**I**	**A**	**S**	**E**	**C**	
High	7	7	7	7	7	7	LETTERS WITH HIGHEST RATINGS
	6	6	6	6	6	6	
	5	5	5	5	5	5	□ 1st
Average	4	4	4	4	4	4	
	3	3	3	3	3	3	□ 2nd
	2	2	2	2	2	2	
Low	1	1	1	1	1	1	□ 3rd
	Manual Skills	Math Ability	Musical Ability	Friend- liness	Managerial Skills	Office Skills	

2. Connect your self-ratings with lines so that you have two line graphs.

3. Each of the six columns in these graphs is labeled with a bold-face letter (between the two graphs). Print the letters for the columns with your three highest rankings in the boxes to the right of each graph. If you rated yourself highest on R, then print an R in the first box, and so on. If your highest ratings on a graph are the same (for example, R = 7, I = 7, E = 6, etc.), rate those traits over again so that there are no ties.

HOW TO ORGANIZE YOUR ANSWERS

1. *Start on page 4.* Count how many times you said L for "Like." Record the number of L's or Y's for each group of *Activities, Competencies,* or *Occupations* in the blank boxes at the end of each group.

2. Plot your letter scores on the graphs below by making a black dot in the appropriate circle for each of your scores, and connect the six dots for each graph with lines.

3. Write down the *letters* for the three highest letter scores. For example, take your "Activities." If letter "R" has the highest number you would put down an "R" first. If "I" has the next highest number, you would put down an "I" in the second box. And if "E" has the next highest number, then put down "E" in the third box.

Note: If high scores are the same or tied, put both letters in the same box separated by a line. For example, if your two highest scores were the same, you might do this: R/I E S. Follow the same procedure if three or more scores are tied, but leave the second and third boxes blank.

Activities Graph (from pages 4 & 5)

LETTERS WITH HIGHEST RATINGS

1st ☐
2nd ☐
3rd ☐

(R)eal   (I)nv   (A)rt   (S)oc   (E)nt   (C)onv

Competencies Graph (from pages 6 & 7)

LETTERS WITH HIGHEST RATINGS

1st ☐
2nd ☐
3rd ☐

(R)eal   (I)nv   (A)rt   (S)oc   (E)nt   (C)onv

Occupations Graph (from page 8)

```
14 ---- o      o       o       o       o       o ----14    LETTERS
         o      o       o       o       o       o          WITH
12 ---- o      o       o       o       o       o ----12    HIGHEST
         o      o       o       o       o       o          RATINGS
10 ---- o      o       o       o       o       o ----10
         o      o       o       o       o       o
 8 ---- o      o       o       o       o       o ---- 8          □ 1st
         o      o       o       o       o       o
 6 ---- o      o       o       o       o       o ---- 6
         o      o       o       o       o       o          □ 2nd
 4 ---- o      o       o       o       o       o ---- 4
         o      o       o       o       o       o
 2 ---- o      o       o       o       o       o ---- 2          □ 3rd
         o      o       o       o       o       o
 0 ---- o      o       o       o       o       o ---- 0
```

(R)eal   (I)nv   (A)rt   (S)oc   (E)nt   (C)onv

HOW MANY TIMES?

Finally, you must obtain your summary code. Review your highest letter scores for the graphs on pages 9 and 10 and the one above. *Be sure to count all five graphs.* Record in the table below the number of times each letter occurs in the first place, how many times each letter occurs in the second place, and how many times each one occurs in the third place in the graphs.

Note: Count any tied scores as separate letters. For example, if you had the letters E, E/I, C, E, C, in the first place for your graphs, you would record 3 E's, 2 C's, and 1I. Treat ties in the second or third positions in the same way.

	1st Place		2nd Place		3rd Place	TOTAL	
R	___ x 3 = □		___ x 2 = □		□ =	___	R
I	___ x 3 = □		___ x 2 = □		□ =	___	I
A	___ x 3 = □		___ x 2 = □		□ =	___	A
S	___ x 3 = □		___ x 2 = □		□ =	___	S
E	___ x 3 = □		___ x 2 = □		□ =	___	E
C	___ x 3 = □		___ x 2 = □		□ =	___	C

Now perform the multiplication and additions indicated in the table. For each letter, multiply the 1st place number by 3, the 2nd place number by 2, and *add the numbers in boxes* all the way across so that you get a number for each letter. The letters with the three highest numbers indicate your summary code. Write your summary code below. (If two scores are the same or tied, put both letters in the same box.)

SUMMARY CODE

□ Highest   □ 2nd   □ 3rd

Go on to page 13

SOME USEFUL BOOKS

Astin, A. W., and Panos, R. J. *The Educational and Vocational Development of College Students*. Washington, D.C.: American Council on Education, 1969. A technical book about the effects of college on student vocational decisions. Also documents the ways students move from field to field in college.

*Crites, J. O. *Vocational Psychology*. New York: McGraw-Hill, 1969. A technical and encyclopedic account of vocational behavior including vocational choice, job satisfaction, and related topics.

Glaser, B. G. *Organizational Careers*. Chicago: Aldine, 1968. A book of readings about careers—theories of, role of motivation, effects of organizations on workers, and other topics.

*Holland, J. L. *The Psychology of Vocational Choice*. Waltham, Massachusetts: Ginn-Blaisdell, 1966. The SDS is based on the theory of personality types and environmental models outlined in this book. Attempts to organize the scientific knowledge of vocational decisions, vocational interests, and personality.

The Occupational Outlook Handbook, U.S. Department of Labor, Bureau of Labor Statistics. This handbook is published every two years and is the best single source for information about occupations. See your counselor or library, or order from Superintendent of Documents, U.S. Government Printing Office, Washington, D.C. 20402, and enclose a check for $6.25.

Roe, Anne. *The Psychology of Occupations*. New York: Wiley, 1956. An interesting account of what we know about people in different occupational groups. Includes Roe's theory of vocational choice and occupational classification.

Super, D. E. *The Psychology of Careers*. New York: Harper, 1957. A useful and readable summary of our occupational knowledge.

Guidance Series Booklets: *Choosing Your Career. Discovering Your Real Interests. How to Get the Job. What Employers Want. Your Personality and Your Job.* Your counselor may have these readable booklets for high school students, or you may order them from Science Research Associates, Chicago, Illinois 60611.

*Available from Consulting Psychologists Press.

Notes:

WHAT YOUR SUMMARY CODE MEANS

The summary code is a simple way of organizing information about people and jobs. Although it is only an estimate, your summary code can be used to discover how your special pattern of interests, self-estimates, and competencies resemble the patterns of interests and competencies that many common occupations demand. In this way, your summary code locates suitable *groups* of occupations for you to consider.

1. Use *The Occupations Finder* and locate the occupations whose codes are *identical* with yours. For instance, if your summary code is I R E, occupations with codes of I R E are *identical* with yours. List some of these occupations below. If you do not find an occupation with an identical code, go to the next paragraph.

Occupation   Education

_____   _____

_____   _____

_____   _____

_____   _____

_____   _____

_____   _____

2. Make a list of occupations whose summary codes *resemble* yours. For instance, if your code is I R E, search *The Occupations Finder* for occupations with all possible arrangements of I R E. Look for occupations with codes of R I E, R E I, I E R, E R I. (If your summary code includes a tie such as R IE A, you must look up more combinations such as R I E, R I A, R E A, etc.) Start by writing down the six possible letter arrangements of your summary code.

Summary Code   Similar Codes

_____   _____ _____ _____ _____ _____

Occupations

_____   _____   _____

_____   _____   _____

_____   _____   _____

_____   _____   _____

_____   _____   _____

_____   _____   _____

SOME NEXT STEPS

1. Compare your summary code with the codes for your Occupational Daydreams on page 3. They should be fairly similar. If they are quite different, you may find it helpful to talk over the differences with a counselor. You should also see a counselor if you do not obtain a satisfactory summary code or if you would like more information.

2. Go back to *The Occupations Finder* and find out how much education or training is required for each of the occupations you listed earlier. Record these facts after each of your occupational possibilities.

3. Seek more information about these occupations from local counseling centers, school counselors, libraries, labor unions, employment services, and occupational information files (usually found in counseling offices).

4. Talk to people employed in the occupations in which you are especially interested. Most business and professional people enjoy talking about their work. Remember, however, that they may have personal biases.

5. Try to obtain part-time work experience that is similar to the activities in the occupation or occupations you are considering, even if you must give your time without pay.

6. Read articles and books that describe occupations or attempt to explain current scientific knowledge about the choice of an occupation. Some suggestions are listed on page 12.

7. Consider any health or physical limitations that might affect your choice.

8. Investigate the educational requirements for the occupations that interest you. Where could you obtain the required training? Is it financially possible? Is it reasonable in terms of your learning ability, age, family situation, etc.

9. Remember: no one but you can make your vocational decision. Our knowledge of vocational choice is too limited to provide you with an exact choice, but we may help you focus on some of the most likely possibilities.

10. Put your SDS workbook away for a few days or weeks. Then get it out and go through it carefully again, changing any answers that should be changed, refiguring your scores and code, reflecting on the results. It is usually best to defer making a single, specific occupational choice until it is absolutely necessary; if one can prepare himself for several related occupations simultaneously, his final selection will have a better chance of fitting his abilities and personality.

Notes:

DUPLICATE SUMMARY PAGE

Your Name_____

Age_____Sex_____Date_____/____/_____

Counselor_____

  You may use this page to provide a copy of your summary sheet for your counselor.

  1. Use *The Occupations Finder* and locate the occupations whose codes are *identical* with yours. For instance, if your summary code is I R E, occupations with codes of I R E are *identical* with yours. List some of these occupations below. If you do not find an occupation with an identical code, go to the next paragraph.

     Occupation   Education

_____ _____

_____ _____

_____ _____

_____ _____

_____ _____

_____ _____

_____ _____

  2. Make a list of occupations whose summary codes *resemble* yours. For instance, if your code is I R E, search *The Occupations Finder* for occupations with all possible arrangements of I R E. Look for occupations with codes of R I E, R E I, I E R, E R I. (If your summary code includes a tie such as R IE A, you must look up more combinations such as R I E, R I A, R E A, etc.) Start by writing down the six possible letter arrangements of your summary code.

Summary Code   Similar Codes

_____ _____ _____ _____ _____ _____

Occupations

_____ _____ _____

_____ _____ _____

_____ _____ _____

_____ _____ _____

_____ _____ _____

_____ _____ _____

The Convergence of
Occupational Codes Obtained
by Different Methods

appendix D

The following table presents the classification codes for only those occupations that were common to all three sources of data (Purdue factors, direct assessment of people with the VPI, or indirect assessment with an alternate form of the VPI applied to Strong data). Note also that we have compared occupations with similar titles and functions as well as occupations with identical titles. A review of this table will usually reveal similar classification codes for the same occupation, although three divergent techniques for the determination of occupational codes have been applied to a variety of divergent, accidental, or convenient samples of both college students and employed adults. No statistical tests were applied to these data because tests appear sensible only for the few identical occupational titles.

NOTE: All VPI codes were obtained from student aspirants unless designated with an "E" for "employee sample." Numbers in parentheses equal sample size. Purdue factors are based on a single job analysis. Two letters underlined indicates ties.

Occupation Category	VPI Data		Purdue Data		Strong Data	
Realistic	Farmer	(149) RIE	Farm laborer	RSE	Farmer	(235) RCS
	Farmer	(190) RIE			Farmer	(77) RCS
					Farmer	(241) RIC
	Electrical worker	(604) RIE	Electrician	RIS	Electrician	(120) RIS
			Electrician	RIE		
			Electrician	RIC		
	Metal/machine worker	(102) RIE	Machinist	RIE	Machinist journeyman	(118) RIS
			Machinist	IRE		
Intellectual	Chemist	(87) IRA	Chemistry inst. tech.	IER	Chemist	(297) IRC
					Chemist	(250) IAR
	Medical technologist	(53) IRS	Head Medical technologist	IES	Medical technologist	(252) ISR
	Medical technologist	(9) IRS				
	Engineering scientist	(44) IRA	Design-div. engineer	IEC	Engineer	(386) IRC
			Research engineer	ICS	Engineer	(1028) IRS
			Design engineer	ICE	Engineer	(93) IRA
	E. Engineer/tech.	(58) IRA			Engineer	(513) IRC
	Engineer	(246) RIE				

Occupation Category	VPI Data		Purdue Data	Strong Data		
Artistic	Music teacher	(63) ASI	Music teacher	SCE	Music teacher	(493) ASI
					Music teacher	(150) ASI
Social	E. counselor	(58) SEI	Voc. rehab. counselor	SEC	Guidance counselor	(44) SIC
	E. counselor	(36) SEA	Voc. rehab. counselor	SEC	Rehab. counselor	(272) SIC
					Guidance counselor	(275) SIC
					School counselor	(203) SIR
	Social worker	(19) SIE	Case worker	SEC	County welfare worker	(55) SCI
	Social service worker	(76) SAE	Case worker	SEC	Social worker	(400) SIA
			Case worker	SEC	Social worker	(54) SIA
			Case worker asst.	SEC		
	E. clergyman	(32) SAI	Chaplain	SEC	Minister	(498) SIA
	E. clergyman	(77) SAI			Minister	(451) SIA
	E. clergyman	(47) SAE			Minister	(60) CSE
					Minister	(151) SAI
					Minister	(293) SIA
					Minister	(97) SAI
					Minister, Unitarian	(113) SAI
					Minister, Unitarian	(69) AIS
					Minister	(250) SAI
	Industrial psychologist	(17) SEA	Industrial psychologist	SEI	Psychologist industrial	(108) ISA
	Secretary	(1024) SCA	Secretary	CRE	Office worker	(326) CIE
	Secretary	(267) SCA	Secretary	CRE	YMCA secretary	(113) SCI

Occupation Category	VPI Data		Purdue Data		Strong Data	
Social			Secretary (N = 3)	CIS	YMCA secretary	(184) SIAC
			Secretary (N = 1)	CIE		
			Secretary (N = 1)	CIR		
			Secretary (N = 6)	CSE		
			Secretary (N = 8)	CSE		
Enterprising	Buyer	(16) ECR	Purchasing agent	ECS	Buyer	(158) ECS
					Buyer	(33) ECI
					Buyer	(41) EIC
					Buyer	(176) ESC
					Purchasing agent	(164) RIE
					Purchasing agent	(219) CIE
	Manager/admin.	(360) ECS	Admin. asst.	ECS	Sales mgr.	(228) EIC
	Manager/admin.	(1178) ECS	Manager	EIS	Sales mgr.	(199) ESI
			Manager (N = 3)	ESC	Dept. store mgr.	(254) ESI
			Manager (N = 11)	ESC		
			Manager (N = 3)	ESI		
Conventional	Accountant	(605) CES	Jr. accountant	CRI	Accountant	(126) ICS
	Accountant	(279) CER	Accounting asst.	CRI	CPA	(304) ICS
			Bookkeeper	CIS	CPA	(612) ICR
					CPA	(354) ICS
					Accountant	(345) CIS

How to Translate
Holland Codes into DOT Codes
or Vice-versa

appendix E

      Many persons will want to search for all the occupations that correspond to their SDS Summary Code. Other persons will want to know what SDS code corresponds to an occupation not listed in the Occupations Finder (SDS). To cope with these questions, two tables have been prepared so that SDS codes can be converted into DOT codes, and DOT codes can be converted into SDS codes.

      Table A-1 shows how any SDS code can be translated into all equivalent occupations in the Dictionary of Occupational Titles. Table A-2 shows how any occupation in the DOT can be translated into an SDS code. Tables A-1 and A-2 come from Viernstein's study (1972), in which the Holland occupational classification was extended to all occupations in the DOT. Although her study was empirical, it should be remembered that these translations are not precise and should be regarded as useful approximations.

      NOTE: Underlining in codes such as 74—means all occupations with codes ranging from 740 to 749. DOT codes are for the first 3 digits.

TABLE E-1

Going from SDS or Holland Codes to DOT Codes

Realistic

RIA	017, 712, 74_
RIS	040, 305, 313, 314, 315, 44_, 52_, 601, 614, 631, 710, 713, 820, 950
RIE	005, 007, 010, 019, 193, 500, 501, 502, 600, 605, 611, 612, 615, 616, 617, 619, 62_, 638, 639, 704, 80_, 821, 822, 823, 824, 825, 826, 862, 863, 864, 865, 866, 89_, 953, 954, 955, 956, 957, 959
RIC	013, 014, 222, 36_, 378, 40_, 411, 412, 419, 42_, 45_, 46_, 503, 504, 505, 509, 54_, 550, 551, 552, 553, 554, 555, 556, 557, 559, 56_, 57_, 59_, 602, 603, 604, 606, 607, 609, 613, 630, 632, 64_, 65_, 66_, 67_, 690, 691, 692, 700, 701, 703, 705, 706, 709, 711, 714, 715, 716, 719, 720, 721, 723, 724, 725, 726, 727, 728, 729, 73_, 75_, 76_, 77_, 81_, 827, 828, 829, 860, 919, 93_, 951, 952, 974, 975
RAI	194, 693, 973, 977
RSE	198, 224, 303, 309, 311, 316, 319, 330, 372, 373, 51_, 610, 913, 915, 922
RSC	240, 317, 318, 371, 38_, 929
RSI	683, 684, 685
REC	302, 306, 686, 689
REI	223, 53_, 637, 869
RES	307, 375, 376, 377, 379, 413, 43_, 910, 912, 920
RCI	018, 304, 633, 694, 699, 79_, 840, 841, 843, 845, 849, 94_, 960
RCS	233, 239, 34_, 558, 680, 681, 682, 78_, 842, 844, 85_, 861, 911
RCE	301, 58_, 90_, 914, 921

Investigative

IAS	
IAR	021, 023, 055
ISC	
ISR	049, 071, 078
ISA	070
IES	074
ICR	199
ICS	
ICE	
IRA	015, 020, 022, 024, 025, 029
IRS	041, 073
IRE	002, 003, 006, 008, 011, 072
IRC	196, 722

Artistic

ASE	150, 151
ASI	149, 152
AES	159, 164, 165, 961, 969

TABLE E-1 (Continued)

AIS	13_,141, 142
AIE	298
AIR	001, 143, 144, 148, 970, 971, 972, 976, 979
ASC	333
AEI	962, 963, 964

Social

SEC	045, 166, 310, 312, 334, 335, 338
SER	241, 26_, 270, 271, 273, 274, 275, 276, 277
	324
SEI	052, 278
SEA	283
SCE	187, 358
SRI	096, 353, 355, 356
SRE	097, 099, 153, 320, 321, 323, 329, 357, 359
SRC	
SIA	054, 059, 075, 090
SIE	077, 168
SIC	195
SIR	079
SAE	091
SAC	331, 332, 339
SAI	051, 092, 094, 10_, 12_, 354

Enterprising

ECR	
ECI	050
ECS	162, 25_,
ERI	182
ERS	
ERC	181
EIS	284
EIR	197
EAS	11_,
EAR	
ESC	163, 169, 180, 183, 184, 186, 188, 189, 191,
	281, 290, 291, 293, 294, 296, 297, 299
ESR	280, 286, 292, 350, 351
ESI	012, 185, 282
ESA	285, 287, 289, 352

Conventional

CRI	207, 208, 229
CRS	206, 234, 236
CRE	221, 231, 232
CIS	160, 213, 214, 215, 217, 219
CIE	202, 203, 209
CIR	216
CSE	201, 204, 205, 235, 237
CSR	230
CSI	210, 211, 212
CSA	242, 243, 249
CER	
CEI	
CES	161

TABLE E-2

Going from DOT Codes to SDS or Holland Codes

DOT Groups	HOC	DOT Groups	HOC	DOT Groups	HOC
001	AIR	12	SAI	2	CSI
2	IRE	13	AIS	3	CIS
3	IRE	141	AIS	4	CIS
5	RIE	2	AIS	5	CIS
6	IRE	3	AIR	6	CIR
7	RIE	4	AIR	7	CIS
8	IRE	8	AIR	9	CIS
010	RIE	9	ASI	221	CRE
1	IRE	150	ASE	2	RIC
2	ESI	1	ASE	3	REI
3	RIC	2	ASI	4	RSE
4	RIC	3	SRE	9	CRI
5	IRA	9	AES	230	CSR
7	RIA	160	CIS	1	CRE
8	RCI	1	CES	2	CRE
9	RIE	2	ECS	3	RCS
020	IRA	3	ESC	4	CRS
1	IAR	4	AES	5	CSE
2	IRA	5	AES	6	CRS
3	IAR	6	SEC	7	CSE
4	IRA	8	SIE	9	RCS
5	IRA	9	ESC	240	RSC
9	IRA	180	ESC	1	SER
040	RIS	1	ERC	2	CSA
1	IRS	2	ERI	3	CSA
5	SEC	3	ESC	9	CSA
9	ISR	4	ESC	25	ECS
050	ECI	5	ESI	26	SER
1	SAI	6	ESC	270	SER
2	SEI	7	SCE	1	SER
4	SIA	8	ESC	3	SER
5	IAR	9	ESC	4	SER
9	SIA	191	ESC	5	SER
070	ISA	3	RIE	6	SER
1	ISR	4	RAI	7	SER
2	IRE	5	SIC	8	SEI
3	IRS	6	IRC	280	ESR
4	IES	7	EIR	1	ESC
5	SIA	8	RSE	2	ESI
7	SIE	9	ICR	3	SEA
8	ISR	201	CSE	4	EIS
9	SIR	2	CIE	5	ESA
090	SIA	3	CIE	6	ESR
1	SAE	4	CSE	7	ESA
2	SAI	5	CSE	9	ESA
4	SAI	6	CRS	290	ESC
6	SRI	7	CRI	1	ESC
7	SRE	8	CRI	2	ESR
9	SRE	9	CIE	3	ESC
10	SAI	210	CSI	4	ESC
11	EAS	1	CSI	6	ESC

TABLE E-2 (Continued)

DOT Groups	HOC	DOT Groups	HOC	DOT Groups	HOC
7	ESC	8	RIC	5	RIE
8	AIE	9	RES	6	RIE
9	ESC	38	RSC	7	RIE
301	RCE	40	RIC	9	RIE
2	REC	411	RIC	62	RIE
3	RSE	2	RIC	630	RIC
4	RCI	3	RES	1	RIS
5	RIS	9	RIC	2	RIC
6	REC	42	RIC	3	RCI
7	RES	43	RES	7	REI
9	RSE	44	RIS	8	RIE
310	SEC	45	RIC	9	RIE
1	RSE	46	RIC	64	RIC
2	SEC	500	RIE	65	RIC
3	RIS	1	RIE	66	RIC
4	RIS	2	RIE	67	RIC
5	RIS	3	RIC	680	RCS
6	RSE	4	RIC	1	RCS
7	RSC	5	RIC	2	RCS
8	RSC	9	RIC	3	RSI
9	RSE	51	RSE	4	RSI
320	SRE	52	RIS	5	RSI
1	SRE	53	REI	6	REC
3	SRE	54	RIC	9	REC
4	SER	550	RIC	690	RIC
9	SRE	1	RIC	1	RIC
330	RSE	2	RIC	2	RIC
1	SAC	3	RIC	3	RAI
2	SAC	4	RIC	4	RCI
3	ASC	5	RIC	9	RCI
4	SEC	6	RIC	700	RIC
5	SEC	7	RIC	1	RIC
8	SEC	8	RCS	3	RIC
9	SAC	9	RIC	4	RIE
34	RCS	56	RIC	5	RIC
350	ESR	57	RIC	6	RIC
1	ESR	58	RCE	9	RIC
2	ESA	59	RIC	710	RIS
3	SRI	600	RIE	1	RIC
4	SAI	1	RIS	2	RIA
5	SRI	2	RIC	3	RIS
6	SRI	3	RIC	4	RIC
7	SRE	4	RIC	5	RIC
8	SCE	5	RIE	6	RIC
9	SRE	6	RIC	9	RIC
361	RIC	7	RIC	720	RIC
371	RSC	9	RIC	1	RIC
2	RSE	610	RSE	2	IRC
3	RSE	1	RIE	3	RIC
5	RES	2	RIE	4	RIC
6	RES	3	RIC	5	RIC
7	RES	4	RIS	6	RIC

TABLE E-2 (Continued)

DOT Groups	HOC	DOT Groups	HOC	DOT Groups	HOC
7	RIC	4	RCS	94	RCI
8	RIC	5	RCI	950	RIS
9	RIC	9	RCI	1	RIC
73	RIC	85	RCS	2	RIC
74	RIA	860	RIC	3	RIE
75	RIC	1	RCS	4	RIE
76	RIC	2	RIE	5	RIE
77	RIC	3	RIE	6	RIE
78	RCS	4	RIE	7	RIE
79	RCI	5	RIE	9	RIE
80	RIE	6	RIE	960	RCI
81	RIC	9	REI	1	AES
820	RIS	89	RIE	2	AEI
1	RIE	90	RCE	3	AEI
2	RIE	910	RES	4	AEI
3	RIE	1	RCS	9	AES
4	RIE	2	RES	970	AIR
5	RIE	3	RSE	1	AIR
6	RIE	4	RCE	2	AIR
7	RIC	5	RSE	3	RAI
8	RIC	9	RIC	4	RIC
9	RIC	920	RES	5	RIC
840	RCI	1	RCE	6	AIR
1	RCI	2	RSE	7	RAI
2	RCS	9	RSC	9	AIR
3	RCI	93	RIC		

Note: Teachers are assigned a code related to the subject they teach; e.g., mathematics teacher has DOT number 091.228, but preferably should be coded using the DOT number for mathematics, 020.088.

Research Suggestions
for Students

appendix F

The following ideas for new research are provided for several reasons: (1) To help students perform better research, (2) to direct them to the more acute research needs, and (3) to help them avoid the sins of others—especially those of the faculty. The ideas outlined here have a single pragmatic orientation. Students will find it helpful to consult other points of view.

SOME HELPFUL PRINCIPLES AND HOMILIES

If you would like to use the theory in your research, you may find it helpful to use the following principles:

1. Read and reread this book until you understand the main ideas. (This will prevent your testing the usefulness of some other theory and will also make you more knowledgeable than your advisor.) If you don't believe the theory makes sense, try testing another.

2. Don't make up your own definitions of the theoretical concepts. This practice is occasionally useful, but it more often leads to the testing of some other theory. If you cannot resist the urge to create new definitions, perhaps you should write another theory. We need more useful theories.

3. Plan your experiment by following the theory as closely as possible. When in doubt, follow the theory whatever its ambiguities. The theory is not intended to be a projective device, although it occasionally serves this function.

4. Avoid deviant populations. It is unlikely that the theory will be useful for understanding people who are mentally retarded, grossly psychotic, and so on. Theories don't have to do everything to be useful.

5. Be selective about your research models. If you see an old research study you like, don't repeat it using new data. Capitalize on its substantive or design strengths, but try to improve the quality of the design, the instrumentation, and so on.

6. Pretend you have your data in hand and everything has come out just as expected. What does it mean? Conduct a thorough run-through of the results with some friends. This kind of review should lead to a more explicit research plan or the abandoning of a bad idea.

7. Write your research report so your father or mother could understand the main ideas. Resist the temptation to impress your advisor or a potential editor with your ability to include every bit of jargon that you've learned in your training.

8. Try to perform the most important study you can within the limits of your resources. Ask yourself whether positive results would make any practical or theoretical difference to anybody. Compare two or more proposals by putting this same question to each.

9. Beware of small Ns. Typological studies usually require large Ns. Small Ns usually restrict the number of analyses you can perform and the number of hypotheses you can cope with.

10. Read the literature. Because only a few people read research reports, you will be at a considerable advantage if you read them.

11. Be clear about "what's the question?" Unless you have a definite idea to test, everything that follows is likely to be unclear: Analyses of data will be unrelated to the question; discussions and conclusions will be ambiguous. If you are clear about the question, then the design, the analysis, and the writing become easier for you and more useful to others.

12. Avoid programmers, methodologists, and statisticians until you are clear about the problem you want to study. They are prone to forget your problem and substitute an elegant analysis of a problem you may not be interested in. Needless to say, they can be helpful, but they must be used as production managers and engineers, not as architects or artists.

13. Spend at least as much time thinking about a potential project as you do fixing your hair or shaving. The quality of research depends more upon daydreaming, thinking, and persistence than upon computers, recording devices, and statistical methods.

NEW RESEARCH

The following sections indicate some research needs and problems that I think are important. These problems are not equally important, nor do they exhaust the major possibilities. Students will be able to think of many more.

Only the questions have been indicated; these require clarification as well as appropriate research plans. And some questions may turn out to be trivial.

Types. The formulations of the personality types suggest numerous questions: Do people assessed as particular types exhibit characteristic interests, competencies, perceptions, and traits? Similarly, do people assessed as particular subtypes exhibit the expected characteristics? What are the most differentiating characteristics of the types? the subtypes?

Do types produce types? Study both parents and their children. Examine the consistency and differentiation of parents and the apparent effects upon children. Consistent and well-differentiated parents should have more predictable influences (friendships and social groupings may follow similar principles). Can you design a study to test the developmental sequence outlined for each type? For example, do activity preferences for science lead to scientific competencies, then to the investigative disposition, and then to specific traits?

Do types search not only for characteristic occupational clusters, but also for characteristic recreational activities, friendships, problems, roles? What happens when searching behavior is blocked or frustrated? Do people then search for closely related (hexagonal model) activities, friends, problems? Does searching behavior become more focused with increasing age? For example, partial reinforcement may lead to more and more precise searching behavior as a person narrows the range of activities and persons he finds rewarding.

Do types perceive occupations in terms of the typological formulations—activities, competencies, perceptions, values, traits? Do types perceive similar types more accurately than dissimilar types? More differentially? What is the effect of training and other experience on a type's ability to perceive other types?

Compare the predictive validity of a person's vocational choice categorized according to type with the Strong, the SDS, the VPI, and so on. See reports and comment by Dolliver (1969), Holland and Lutz (1968), Campbell (1968), and Richards (1970) before you start. Compare the predictive validity of a person's history of daydreams or work history with the same devices. Compare the work histories of the same types, all six types, or the work histories of the same subtypes or selected subtypes. Different types should have characteristic work histories.

Test the hypotheses about level of occupational achievement using adult work histories. Compare the work histories of people in *Who's Who* or other biographical references with the histories of average adults. Compare the work histories of people in special fields of science, education, business, and so on. Code, interpret, and summarize the work histories of the members of your state legislature or the U.S. Congress. Some federal agencies such as the Office of Education publish organizational charts. Code, interpret, and summarize the work histories of people at each level of this vast bureaucracy. Try the same procedure on other organizations. Perform a longitudinal study of an organization by studying the organizational charts at different times.

Environments. Using the Environmental Assessment Technique (EAT), assess educational or occupational environments and compare the EAT with other environmental assessment techniques such as CUES. Explore ways to map relatively independent subenvironmental units. Identify the major environmental influences—size, power, educational level, and so on—that the EAT does not account for; then develop and test research designs to cope with this problem. See if you can improve the EAT by incorporating Barker and Gump's concept (1964) of behavior setting and size. Plan a study and test your ideas. Select a particular population and code all the environments that population lives in. Try to segregate the environments that form each person's psychological field. Examine these environmental data for their consistency. Analyze life histories in terms of environments only: relatives as environments, teachers as environments, and so on. Assess neighborhoods as environments and map a city or county according to the types of the heads of households (a city directory can be used for this purpose).

Interactions. Study the following kinds of interactions: student-teacher, parent-child, counselor-client, employee-supervisor, man-wife, child-child, and so on. Observe the following cautions in the study of interactions:

1. Examine the character of the interaction—amount of time, intensity, involvement, nature of task, degree of risk.
2. Define the degree of congruence carefully. Use the Cole planar method or the hexagonal model.
3. Assess the subject's perception of the interaction (is he involved?).
4. Use your judgment. Rule out some interactions as tangential and rule others in as central.
5. Incorporate the degrees of consistency and differentiation of both persons and environments in your design.
6. Look for linear and nonlinear interactions.

In general, test hypotheses as analytically as possible: (1) study *individual* permutations (combining of permutations—such as RIs plus RSs plus REs—hides information). (2) Control for environmental opportunity and type of person—for example, RIs vs. RSs, or ESs vs. EAs, and so on. And (3) determine the reliability of outcome or dependent variables.

Classification. Use the classification to organize and interpret work histories, census data, and occupational aspirations. Use the Cole planar method or the hexagonal model to determine if friendships are related to the actual distance between types; if aspirational and work histories are in accord with the hexagonal model. Test the limits of the classification: For instance, are RIEs different than RISs, and are the differences according to the formulations for Es and Ss? Why do some subcategories such as CA, AC, and so on never occur among the occupational codes and rarely occur in SDS or VPI profiles? Try some cross-cultural comparisons of work forces. Do the differences appear consistent with sociological and anthropological interpretations of national character?

Develop codes for occupations previously unclassified, check the validity of the categorization of selected occupations by testing employed samples, compare occupational samples to see if they possess the characteristics that the classification attributes to them.

Hexagonal model. Explore the usefulness of the hexagonal model for defining consistency and congruence. For example, suppose consistency equals the area of the triangle formed inside the hexagon by a person's three-letter code. Test some hypotheses about the effects of consistency using both definitions (the present definition and the areal definition). Are finer definitions using three or four letters of congruence desirable and do they result in more useful distinctions?

Differentiation. Does it help to distinguish the various profile patterns having the same degree of differentiation? For example, two profiles may have the same differentiation score (the same high and low points), but different intervening scales. Both may have R and A as the highest and lowest scales, but they could have codes of RIE and REC, respectively. Other possibilities occur—two profiles may have identical differentiation scores, but have no high or low codes in common. A resolution of these possibilities and problems would be especially helpful.

Index